VERDURE!

Vegetables the Italian Way

VERDURE!

Vegetables the Italian Way

Text by Elisabetta Lotti
Photography by Marco Lanza
Set Design by Elisabetta Lotti

Other titles in the same series:
Pastissima! Pasta the Italian Way
Antipasti Appetisers the Italian Way
Zuppe, Risotto e Polenta Italian Soup, Risotto and Polenta Dishes

© McRae Books 1997

Conceived, edited and designed by McRae Books, Florence, Italy

Text: Elisabetta Lotti
Photography: Marco Lanza
Set Design: Elisabetta Lotti

Design: Marco Nardi
Translation from the Italian: Executive Service
Editing: Alison Leach

The Publishers would like to thank Bartolini (Fiesole) and Coin (Florence)
for their assistance during the production of this book

Color separations: Fotolito Toscana, Florence, Italy
Printed and bound in Italy by Grafiche Editoriali Padane, Cremona
ISBN 88-900126-3-3

Contents

INTRODUCTION

Every season brings its harvest of fresh, life-giving vegetables. Cooking and preparing them for family and friends is always satisfying. Not only will the results of your labours be greeted with pleasure and healthy appetites, but you will be serene in the knowledge that you are doing your guests a good turn. Vegetables are overflowing with essential vitamins, minerals, and fibre, and along with fruit, should be one of the mainstays of a healthy diet. Fortunately, Italy's Mediterranean climate ensures a well-stocked vegetable cupboard year round, and its long and justly famous culinary tradition contains a rich store of recipes for all seasons and every occasion.

To introduce even novice cooks to a part of this tradition, I have divided the book into five chapters based on the ways the vegetables are prepared, preceded by an introductory section on recognising and choosing vegetables, preparing and cooking them, and the basic utensils and sauces required. Most recipes finish with one or more serving suggestions. These are only intended as guidelines; all the dishes in this book can be served in myriad ways. Experiment a little, and find them all out! Buon appetito!

Types of Vegetables

For those of us without green fingers or a garden, the vegetables we eat will be bought at a greengrocer, supermarket or market. If you have the choice, buy at a market where the vegetables will be fresher. In Italy, small farmers bring their products into the market squares fresh from the fields every morning, which is almost as good as having your own garden! When buying vegetables, quality and freshness are of utmost importance. Generally speaking, products should be firm to touch, with good colour, and no withered or yellowing leaves. Experience is the best guide, so examine the vegetables you buy closely to learn what each one should look like to taste good. Another important rule is that all vegetables need to be very thoroughly washed in abundant cold running water before you begin preparing them.

ARTICHOKES

Choose artichokes with plump heads and tightly folded leaves. Young artichokes can be eaten raw; the maturer ones are better cooked. Only the inner leaves and heart are edible. To clean an artichoke, remove all but the pale inner leaves by pulling the outer ones down and snapping them off. Cut off the stem at the base of the head and the top third of the leaves. Cut the artichokes in half lengthwise and scrape any fuzzy choke away with a knife. Soak them in a bowl of cold water with the juice of 1 lemon for 10 minutes to stop them turning black.

ASPARAGUS

The asparagus season is mid-spring to early summer, although nowadays speciality markets keep imported ones all year round. Often expensive, it pays to choose them with care. They should be firm, with well-formed, compact spears. Beware of wilting spears or woody stems. Asparagus should be cooked and eaten as soon as possible. Trim the tough parts off the stems, wash well, and cook in (or steam over) a pot of salted, boiling water until tender.

GREEN BEANS

Also known as French beans, they are best in spring and summer. They should be bright green with no blemishes or spots. Snap the end off one between your thumb and forefinger; if fresh, the bean will break easily. To prepare, cut the ends off and wash well.

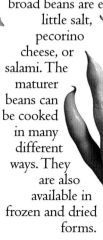

PEAS

Fresh green peas appear in the markets in spring and summer. The younger they are, the sweeter they will be. Choose those with plump, bright green pods. They should be eaten as soon as possible. During the rest of the year frozen peas are an acceptable substitute and widely available.

BROAD BEANS

Broad beans are in season from early spring to mid-summer. Buy them when their pods are bright green and crisp. In Italy, very young broad beans are eaten raw with a little salt, pecorino cheese, or salami. The maturer beans can be cooked in many different ways. They are also available in frozen and dried forms.

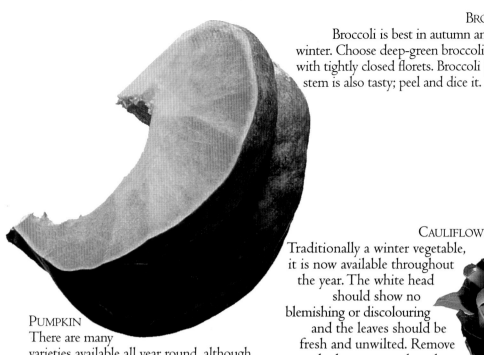

BROCCOLI

Broccoli is best in autumn and winter. Choose deep-green broccoli with tightly closed florets. Broccoli stem is also tasty; peel and dice it.

PUMPKIN

There are many varieties available all year round, although they are better in autumn and winter. Often sold in pieces, make sure that they are unblemished, with no soft spots. If buying a whole pumpkin, choose one with a glossy skin which feels heavy. Pumpkin keeps in the refrigerator for several days.

CAULIFLOWER

Traditionally a winter vegetable, it is now available throughout the year. The white head should show no blemishing or discolouring and the leaves should be fresh and unwilted. Remove the leaves to cook and divide the head into florets. The stalk is also tasty but takes longer to cook than the florets. Peel it, dice it up, and add to the pot 5 minutes before the florets.

COURGETTES (ZUCCHINI)

Their natural season is spring to autumn, although they are now available all year round. Courgettes should be firm to touch, with glossy, blemish-free skins. They are at their peak in early summer and can be eaten raw then. In Italy, courgette blossoms are considered a delicacy. Buy the male flowers that grow on a stem, and not the female ones which are attached to the end of the courgette. The blossoms are usually dipped in batter (see recipe p. 24) and fried for a few minutes in oil. Sprinkled with salt, they make a tasty appetiser. Sprinkled with sugar, they are a delicious dessert.

CABBAGE

There are many different varieties of cabbage, including Savoy, red or the common pale green type. Normally a winter vegetable, some varieties also grow during spring and summer. Most cabbages have tightly packed leaves and will keep in the refrigerator for 4-5 days. Remove the tough stem and wilted outer leaves and cut or chop the vegetable as required. Cabbage can be eaten raw, or cooked in a variety of ways.

BRUSSELS SPROUTS

These tiny cabbages grow in autumn and winter. Buy them fresh, firm, and bright green in colour. They will keep for 2-3 days in the refrigerator in a plastic bag. Trim the stems, remove the outer leaves, and rinse thoroughly under cold running water. Cook them in salted, boiling water for 7-8 minutes. Don't overcook or they will turn mushy and tasteless.

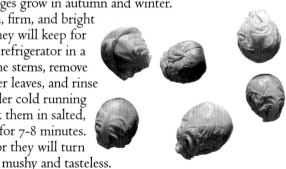

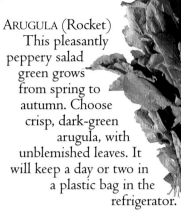

SALAD BURNET

One of the many small salad greens commonly available in Italy. Lamb's lettuce, cress, wild endives, and lollo rosso are also popular. Choose local varieties of crisp, fresh greens.

SPINACH

Available from autumn to spring. Choose young, tender spinach with crisp, deep-green leaves. Separate the leaves and wash very thoroughly. Frozen spinach is an acceptable substitute in summer.

ARUGULA (Rocket)

This pleasantly peppery salad green grows from spring to autumn. Choose crisp, dark-green arugula, with unblemished leaves. It will keep a day or two in a plastic bag in the refrigerator.

ESCAROLE

Another member of the chicory family. Buy escarole only when it its open wavy leaves, with their pale-green ruffled tips, are crisp and unwilted. The heart can be used in salads, while the leaves have a pleasant, earthy taste when cooked.

RADICCHIO

There are several types of round or long red radicchio available in Italy throughout the year. They are all more or less bitter in taste and can be served either raw in salads, or baked or grilled. There are also many varieties of small green radicchio (both wild and cultivated) available in Italy. They are usually served in salads.

BELGIAN ENDIVE

Also known as French endive. Another member of the chicory family. Choose white, well-closed heads and store them in the dark – the light will turn the leaves green. Clean by removing the outer leaves and chopping the tough part off the bottom. Serve in salads or cooked.

CATALONIA

Part of the chicory family, this is a bitter cooking green with long, tapering leaves, white at the bottom and dark green towards the tops. Choose compact, unwilted heads. If you enjoy bracing bitter flavours, serve it boiled or steamed, dressed with a little olive oil and lemon juice.

LETTUCE

There are many different types of lettuce available throughout the year. Common cutting lettuce is usually round, with pale green and white leaves folded over each other. The central white heart is the best part. Cos lettuce has elongated dark green leaves. Choose lettuces with crisp well-coloured leaves. Trim the bottoms, detach the leaves and wash accurately.

SWISS CHARD (SILVER BEET)

The dwarf varieties are sweeter and lack the large white stalk of the larger ones. They can be served raw in salads or cooked. The large stalks are nearly always cooked. Choose fresh, bright green heads with crisp leaves.

ONIONS

There are many types of onions available throughout the year. The large white and yellow varieties are used to flavour many cooked dishes, while the large red variety is sweet enough to be served (thinly sliced) in salads. Squeeze onions before you buy them to make sure they are not rotting beneath their skins.

BABY ONIONS

White, baby onions can be pickled, grilled or served in sweet and sour sauces.

LEEKS

A member of the onion family. Trim off the green tops and roots, and peel the outer layers of the central white stalk. Although sometimes served in salads, their strong flavour makes them more suitable for cooking. Buy them with their green tops, which should be fresh-looking and unwilted.

SPRING ONIONS

Available from early spring to autumn. Trim the tops and bottoms, peel off the outer layers of white skin, and chop into salads.

FENNEL

With its mild taste of aniseed, fennel is a refreshing salad vegetable. It can also be braised, sautéed, baked or fried. Only the bulb is used; the stalks and leaves are usually discarded. Available year round, its natural season is winter and spring. Generally speaking, the plump bulbs are best in salads, while the longer, flatter ones are better cooked.

CELERY

Choose fresh, crisp heads of celery with bright white stalks and unwilted green leaves. Use only the inner stalks and hearts in salads. To cook, remove the strings from the larger, outer stalks before chopping.

CARDOONS

Cardoons taste like artichokes, although they look more like a head of celery to buy. Choose crisp, unwilted heads. Trim the tops, strip off the outer, bitter-tasting leaves and serve raw or cooked.

RADISHES
Available throughout the year. Try to buy them with their tops attached, since these will show how fresh they are. Cut off the roots and tops, wash well, and serve the tiny red bulbs in salads, or by themselves (with a dish of salt handy for dipping).

CARROTS
Carrots are available throughout the year. Baby carrots are often sold with their tops; if the leaves are bright green and unwilted the carrots will be fresh. Choose older carrots carefully; they should be bright orange in colour, well-shaped, and firm. Scrub well or peel before use.

CHERRY TOMATOES
In season, tiny cherry tomatoes are packed with flavour.

TOMATOES
The tomato is ubiquitous in Italian cuisine. Fresh tomatoes are now available year round, although the outdoor, summer varieties have an unbeatable taste. Tinned tomatoes are an acceptable substitute for fresh ones in sauces and soups during the winter months.

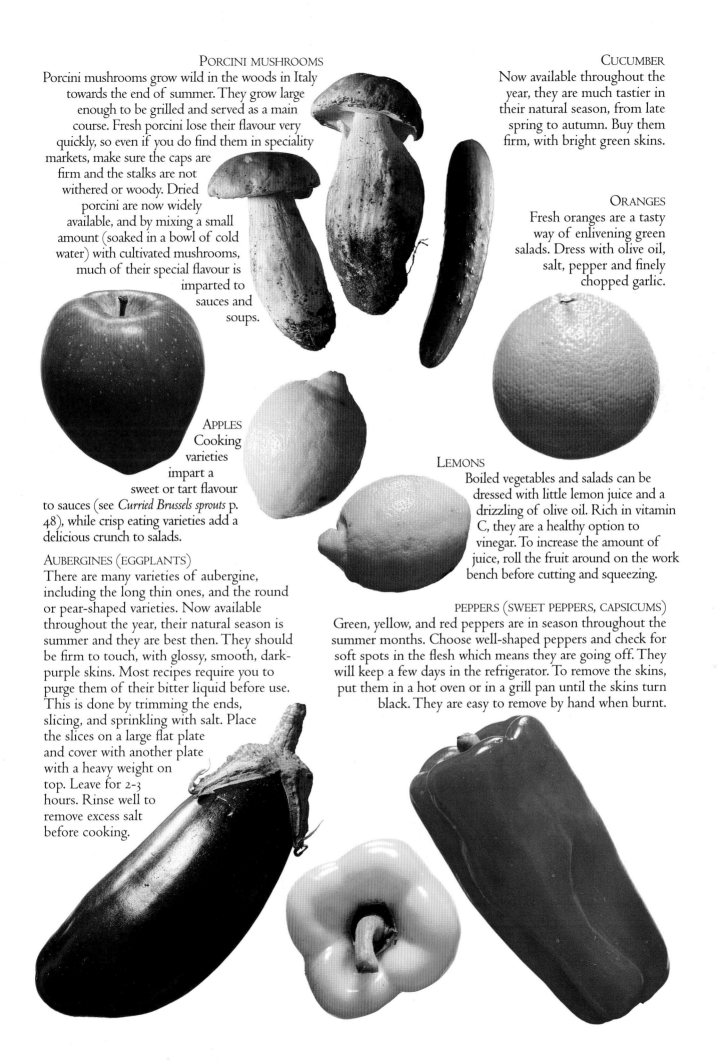

PORCINI MUSHROOMS

Porcini mushrooms grow wild in the woods in Italy towards the end of summer. They grow large enough to be grilled and served as a main course. Fresh porcini lose their flavour very quickly, so even if you do find them in speciality markets, make sure the caps are firm and the stalks are not withered or woody. Dried porcini are now widely available, and by mixing a small amount (soaked in a bowl of cold water) with cultivated mushrooms, much of their special flavour is imparted to sauces and soups.

CUCUMBER

Now available throughout the year, they are much tastier in their natural season, from late spring to autumn. Buy them firm, with bright green skins.

ORANGES

Fresh oranges are a tasty way of enlivening green salads. Dress with olive oil, salt, pepper and finely chopped garlic.

APPLES

Cooking varieties impart a sweet or tart flavour to sauces (see *Curried Brussels sprouts* p. 48), while crisp eating varieties add a delicious crunch to salads.

LEMONS

Boiled vegetables and salads can be dressed with little lemon juice and a drizzling of olive oil. Rich in vitamin C, they are a healthy option to vinegar. To increase the amount of juice, roll the fruit around on the work bench before cutting and squeezing.

AUBERGINES (EGGPLANTS)

There are many varieties of aubergine, including the long thin ones, and the round or pear-shaped varieties. Now available throughout the year, their natural season is summer and they are best then. They should be firm to touch, with glossy, smooth, dark-purple skins. Most recipes require you to purge them of their bitter liquid before use. This is done by trimming the ends, slicing, and sprinkling with salt. Place the slices on a large flat plate and cover with another plate with a heavy weight on top. Leave for 2-3 hours. Rinse well to remove excess salt before cooking.

PEPPERS (SWEET PEPPERS, CAPSICUMS)

Green, yellow, and red peppers are in season throughout the summer months. Choose well-shaped peppers and check for soft spots in the flesh which means they are going off. They will keep a few days in the refrigerator. To remove the skins, put them in a hot oven or in a grill pan until the skins turn black. They are easy to remove by hand when burnt.

Herbs, Spices and Cooking Tips

Fresh herbs will add extra zest and flavour to everything you cook, whether it be Italian or not. Most common herbs are now readily available at markets. If you can't find fresh herbs, use them in dried form. Remember to store dried herbs in airtight containers and to buy new supplies regularly, so that they don't lose all their flavour.

BASIL

MINT

CHERVIL

HOW TO GRILL VEGETABLES

Grilling vegetables is a traditional cooking method in Italy. For best results indoors, you will need a basic grill pan (see p. 19). You can also successfully grill vegetables over a barbecue, in the same way that meat is cooked. The most suitable vegetables are bell peppers, aubergine (eggplant), mushrooms, red radicchio, courgettes (zucchini), fennel, tomatoes, and onions.

There are only two basic rules:

• Choose only top quality vegetables for grilling.

• Temperature: heat the grill pan to very hot before placing the vegetables in it. This stops them from sticking to the pan and cooks them quickly (so that they won't have time to dry out).

And many advantages:

• Simplicity and speed: the vegetables only need to be washed and chopped. You can grill a good selection of vegetables in about 30 minutes. The result will be an attractive and delicious first course or side dish for 4-6 people.

• Health: grilling vegetables not only enhances their natural flavours, it also maintains most of their vitamins and minerals intact.

• Low fat: the vegetables are grilled without oil, butter, or fats of any kind. You can choose how much oil to add when serving.

• Preparing ahead of time: when the vegetables are grilled, you can either drizzle with olive oil and serve them hot, or let cool and sprinkle with freshly chopped herbs (garlic, parsley, mint, oregano, and others). Dress with oil and serve later in the day. Well-covered with oil, peppers and aubergine will keep for about a week in the refrigerator.

FLAT-LEAF
PARSLEY

TARRAGON

DILL

CHIVES

HOW TO FRY VEGETABLES

To obtain perfect results when frying vegetables you will need a deep-sided frying pan or sauté pan, a slotted spoon, tongs (or two forks), and abundant high-quality oil. Fried dishes should be eaten hot; serve them as you cook or as soon afterwards as possible. Prepare the vegetables and batter beforehand. Basic rules for successful frying are:

• Oil: olive oil is one of the best oils for frying. It resists heat well and leaves no taste on the food. Sunflower oil is also good.

• Temperature: don't begin frying before the oil is hot enough. Initially, you may prefer to use a thermometer to gauge heat. Ideal cooking temperatures are:
Medium 140°C-150°C (275°F-300°F): ideal for larger pieces of raw vegetable that need time to cook;
Hot 150°C-160°C (300°F-325°F): ideal for precooked vegetables and croquettes;
Very hot 160°C-180°C (325°F-350°F): ideal for vegetables in julienne strips, leaves, or tiny pieces of vegetables which require instant frying.
Otherwise, check temperature by putting a small piece of the vegetable you wish to fry in the oil to see how it reacts and adjust temperature accordingly. Temperature should never exceed 180°C (350°F). Don't wait until the oil is smoking; this is dangerous as the oil may catch fire (if it does, don't use water to extinguish it, just turn off the electricity or gas and cover the pan with a lid).

• Always use plenty of oil. The vegetables should be floating when you add them to the pan so that their surfaces seal immediately against the oil. The less oil that enters the surface, the lighter and healthier the finished dish will be.

• Never use the same oil more than once. During cooking, keep the oil clean; if you leave tiny pieces of batter or vegetable in the pan, they will burn and their acrid taste will contaminate the taste of the other vegetables. Keep the oil topped up to the same level during cooking.

• The vegetables you want to fry should be at room temperature. If they are too cold, they will take longer to heat and absorb more oil.

• Don't put too many pieces in the pan at once. They will lower the temperature of the oil, increasing cooking time and amount of oil absorbed. They may also stick together in a single unappetising lump.

• If you are using a wire basket, heat it in the oil before adding the vegetables to prevent them from sticking to it.

GARLIC

BLACK PEPPERCORNS

SHALLOTS

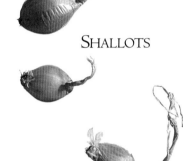

SAGE

CHILLIES

OREGANO

BAY LEAVES   THYME   CALAMINT   ROSEMARY

Meats, Cheeses, Oil and Vinegar

Many of the dishes in this book are prepared using ingredients that are specific to the Italian pantry. Due to the success of Italian cuisine abroad, most are now widely available in supermarkets and food stores. You may need to look for some of the cheeses in speciality stores. If you can't find the exact Italian ingredient, read the description carefully and look for a similar local product. Olive oil is the only ingredient that can't be substituted with another.

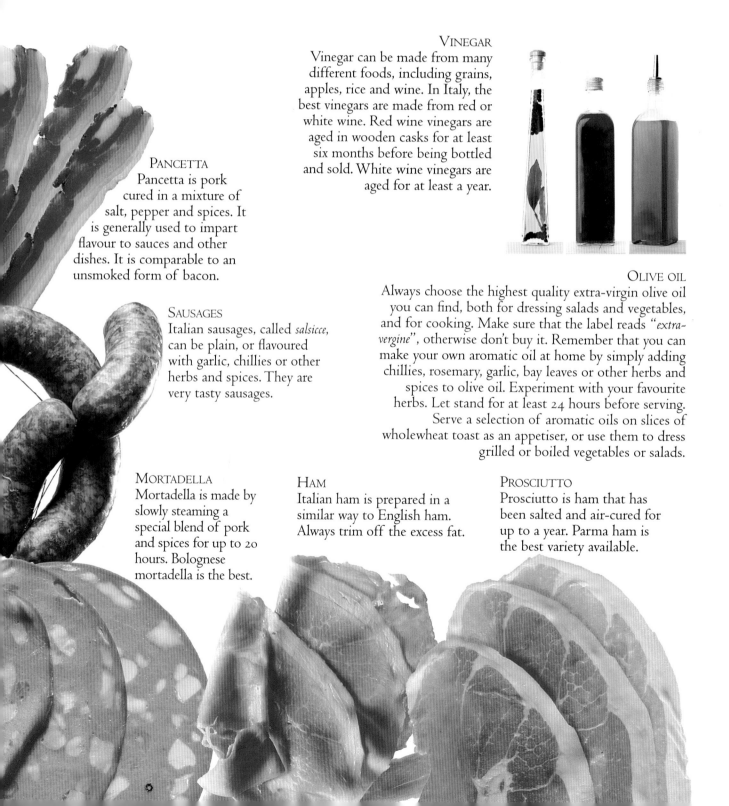

Vinegar
Vinegar can be made from many different foods, including grains, apples, rice and wine. In Italy, the best vinegars are made from red or white wine. Red wine vinegars are aged in wooden casks for at least six months before being bottled and sold. White wine vinegars are aged for at least a year.

Pancetta
Pancetta is pork cured in a mixture of salt, pepper and spices. It is generally used to impart flavour to sauces and other dishes. It is comparable to an unsmoked form of bacon.

Olive oil
Always choose the highest quality extra-virgin olive oil you can find, both for dressing salads and vegetables, and for cooking. Make sure that the label reads *"extra-vergine"*, otherwise don't buy it. Remember that you can make your own aromatic oil at home by simply adding chillies, rosemary, garlic, bay leaves or other herbs and spices to olive oil. Experiment with your favourite herbs. Let stand for at least 24 hours before serving. Serve a selection of aromatic oils on slices of wholewheat toast as an appetiser, or use them to dress grilled or boiled vegetables or salads.

Sausages
Italian sausages, called *salsicce*, can be plain, or flavoured with garlic, chillies or other herbs and spices. They are very tasty sausages.

Mortadella
Mortadella is made by slowly steaming a special blend of pork and spices for up to 20 hours. Bolognese mortadella is the best.

Ham
Italian ham is prepared in a similar way to English ham. Always trim off the excess fat.

Prosciutto
Prosciutto is ham that has been salted and air-cured for up to a year. Parma ham is the best variety available.

FONTINA WEDGE
For the cheese board.

FONTINA
Tasty cheese originally from the Valle d'Aosta in the foothills and Alps of northern Italy. Made from cow's milk, it is ideal both for cooking and the cheese board.

FONTINA SLICES
Ideal for cooking.

MOZZARELLA
Traditionally made from buffalo milk. Many good quality varieties are now made from cow's milk.

MASCARPONE
Made from cow's cream, it is a fresh cheese and will only keep a day or two in the refrigerator.

PROVOLONE
Provolone cheese is made from cow's milk. In Italy it comes in an amazing variety of forms, from tiny pear-like shapes to gigantic cylinders. It has a thin golden brown crust. There are two main types – *dolce* (mild) and *piccante* (tasty). Tasty provolone is ideal for flavouring dishes. Grate over the top as with parmesan or pecorino.

PECORINO
Tasty *pecorino romano*, made from ewe's milk and carefully aged, is best for grating over baked dishes. The younger varieties can be eaten fresh.

PARMIGIANO
Parmesan is made from cow's milk aged for at least 18 months. Buy in wedges and grate fresh as required.

CAPRINO
A delicate, slightly tart fresh cheese made of goat's milk, or a mixture of goat's and cow's milk.

GRUYÈRE AND EMMENTHAL
From Switzerland, France and Holland, they are widely used in Italian cookery.

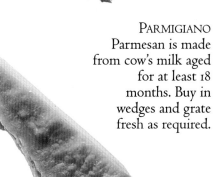

RICOTTA
Delicate fresh cheese made of goat's, ewe's, or cow's milk.

Utensils for Cooking Vegetables

You don't need a lot of special equipment for preparing superb vegetable dishes. An ordinary well-stocked kitchen will already have the basic outlay of pots, pans, choppers and bowls required. The only piece that many English or Australian kitchens may lack will be the grill pan. Grill pans are now widely available in good kitchen-supply stores. Use it to grill meat, fish and sausages, as well as the vegetable dishes in this book.

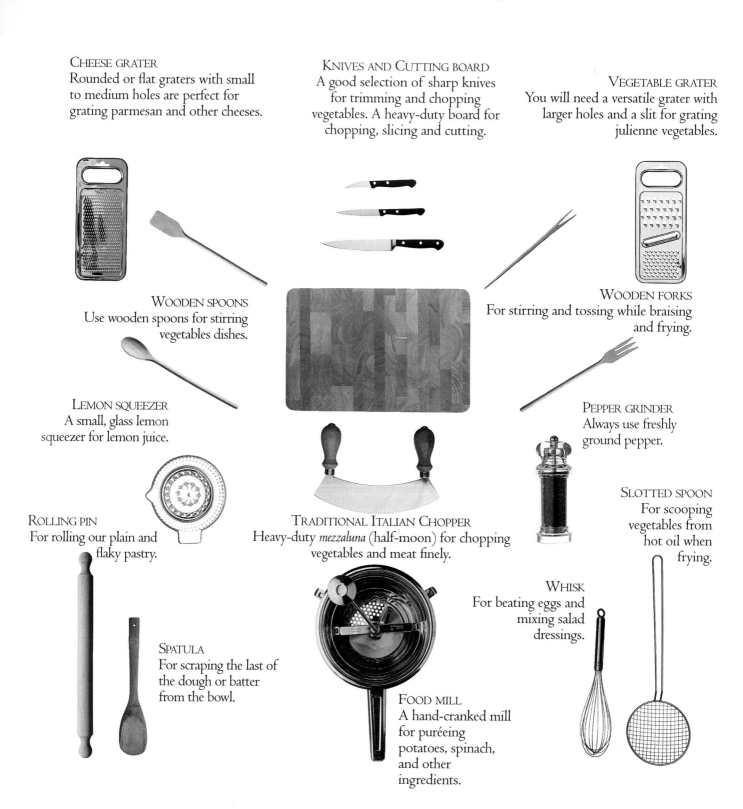

CHEESE GRATER
Rounded or flat graters with small to medium holes are perfect for grating parmesan and other cheeses.

KNIVES AND CUTTING BOARD
A good selection of sharp knives for trimming and chopping vegetables. A heavy-duty board for chopping, slicing and cutting.

VEGETABLE GRATER
You will need a versatile grater with larger holes and a slit for grating julienne vegetables.

WOODEN SPOONS
Use wooden spoons for stirring vegetables dishes.

WOODEN FORKS
For stirring and tossing while braising and frying.

LEMON SQUEEZER
A small, glass lemon squeezer for lemon juice.

PEPPER GRINDER
Always use freshly ground pepper.

ROLLING PIN
For rolling our plain and flaky pastry.

TRADITIONAL ITALIAN CHOPPER
Heavy-duty *mezzaluna* (half-moon) for chopping vegetables and meat finely.

SLOTTED SPOON
For scooping vegetables from hot oil when frying.

SPATULA
For scraping the last of the dough or batter from the bowl.

WHISK
For beating eggs and mixing salad dressings.

FOOD MILL
A hand-cranked mill for puréeing potatoes, spinach, and other ingredients.

Skillet with heat-resistant wood handle.

METAL TONGS
Tongs are useful for picking up and turning vegetables while frying.

Lightweight, aluminium skillet.

FRYING PANS
You will need a selection of heavy-bottomed, shallow-sided frying pans in aluminium, stainless steel, or cast iron for sautéeing.

Nonstick skillet, for crêpes.

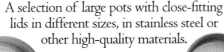

GRILL PAN
A ridged, nonstick grill pan for quick no-fat vegetable cookery.

POTS
A selection of large pots with close-fitting lids in different sizes, in stainless steel or other high-quality materials.

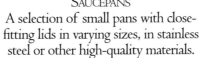

SAUCEPANS
A selection of small pans with close-fitting lids in varying sizes, in stainless steel or other high-quality materials.

BAKING DISH
An ovenproof baking dish with lid. There are some lovely earthenware dishes available, which will give many of your baked vegetable dishes a special earthy flavour.

Ovenproof glass baking dish

SAUTÉ PAN
You will need two or three deep-sided sauté pans for braising and sautéeing vegetables. They should all have close-fitting lids. Buy them in stainless steel or other high-quality materials.

BASIC SAUCES

RAGÙ DI CARNI MISTE
Meat sauce

Ragù is a tomato-based sauce made with meat and chopped vegetables and spices. It is one of the classic pasta sauces, but is also very good with many vegetable recipes, particularly baked dishes. Because making a ragù is a time-consuming business (and also because it will keep in the refrigerator for about a week and in the freezer for several months), the recipe below is for 10-12 portions.

Serves 10-12; Preparation: 1 hour; Cooking: 2½ hours; Level of difficulty: Simple

Place 3 tablespoons of oil, 3 cloves of garlic, the sage, rosemary, beef, pork, chicken and sausages in a large heavy-bottomed pan and cook for 15 minutes, stirring frequently with a wooden spoon. § When the meat is almost cooked (browned, with no red blood visible), remove from the pan, drain and set aside on a plate. § Discard the sage and rosemary and add the carrots, onion, celery and the rest of the garlic and oil. Stir well to amalgamate and cook for 5-10 minutes. § In the meantime, chop the meat finely in an electric blender or with a sharp knife. § Pour the wine over the vegetables and cook for 10 more minutes. § Add the meat and brandy and cook until the brandy evaporates. § Add the milk and simmer for 5 minutes, then add the tomatoes. § Season with salt and pepper, turn the heat to medium-low, and simmer, partially covered, for about 2 hours. § Stir the sauce from time to time so that it doesn't stick to the bottom of the pan. § After 1½ hours, add the basil and taste to see if there is enough salt. § If, after 2 hours, the ragù is too watery, uncover and simmer for 10-15 minutes more. § When cooked, add the butter and remove from the heat.

■ INGREDIENTS

- 250 ml (8fl oz) extra-virgin olive oil
- 5 cloves garlic, finely chopped
- 1 sprig fresh sage
- 2 twigs fresh rosemary
- 300 g (10 oz) lean beef, coarsely chopped
- 400 g (14 oz) lean pork, coarsely chopped
- 1 large chicken breast, boneless and coarsely chopped
- 2 Italian pork sausages, skinned and crumbled
- 2 large carrots, 1 large onion, 2 large stalks celery, all finely chopped
- 300 ml (10fl oz) dry white wine
- 250 ml (8fl oz) brandy
- 650 ml (21fl oz) milk
- 1.8 kg (3½ lb) tinned tomatoes
- salt and freshly ground black pepper
- 40 leaves fresh basil, torn
- 50 g (1½ oz) butter

SALSA DI POMODORO SEMPLICE
Basic tomato sauce

Tomato sauce is another classic for pasta, but it is very versatile and can be used in many other dishes, including those based on vegetables, eggs or meat. If you use fresh tomatoes, you will need to cook the sauce a little longer (about 25 minutes), because of the water they release during cooking. Needless to say, fresh tomatoes produce the tastiest results. Add a knob of butter at the end for a sweeter sauce.

Serves 4; Preparation: 5 minutes; Cooking: 15-20 minutes; Level of difficulty: Simple

Cook the garlic in a sauté pan with the oil until golden, remove from the pan, and add the tomatoes. Season with salt and pepper to taste and cook over medium heat. § Add the basil 5 minutes before the sauce is cooked. § If the sauce is still too watery, turn up the heat until it reduces sufficiently.

■ INGREDIENTS

- 3 cloves garlic, cut in half
- 4 tablespoons extra-virgin olive oil
- 500 g (1 lb) peeled and chopped fresh or tinned tomatoes
- salt and freshly ground black pepper
- 10 leaves fresh basil

Right:
Ragù di carni miste

Pasta frolla salata
Plain pastry

■ INGREDIENTS

- 250 g (8 oz) plain flour
- 1 egg yolk
- pinch of salt
- 125 g (4 oz) butter, softened
- about 125 ml (4fl oz) water, ice cold

Serves 4-6; Preparation: 50 minutes; Level of difficulty: Medium

Sift the flour in a heap on a clean work bench and put the egg yolk, salt and butter in the middle. Using your fingers, begin mixing the ingredients. Gradually work in all the flour, adding water as you go along. If any lumps form, sprinkle them with water and knead the dough with the palms of your hands. § Keep kneading on the floured work surface until the dough is soft but stays together in one piece without sticking to the bench. § Form the dough into a ball, wrap in a clean cotton tea towel and place in the refrigerator for about 40 minutes. § Follow the instructions in each recipe for baking. This recipe will produce enough plain pastry to line a round baking dish 25 cm (10 in) in diameter.

Pasta sfoglia salata
Flaky pastry

■ INGREDIENTS

- 250 g (8 oz) plain flour
- 2 pinches salt
- about 200 ml (7fl oz) water
- 250 g (8 oz) butter, softened

Serves 4-6; Preparation: 1½ hours; Level of difficulty: Medium

Sift the flour and salt in a mound on a clean work bench, make a well in the centre and pour about ¾ of the water into it. Using your hands, mix the ingredients until the dough is the same consistency as the softened butter. Adjust the dough to achieve the required consistency by adding flour or water. § Roll the dough into a ball, wrap it in a clean cotton tea towel and set it aside for 30 minutes. § Use a rolling pin to roll the dough out into a square shape on a floured work bench until about 1 cm (½ in) thick. § Cut the softened butter in pieces and place them at the centre of the square. Fold the 4 sides of the square so that the butter is completely sealed in and roll the dough out in a rectangular shape about 1 cm (½ in) thick. § Fold the rectangle in 3, turn the folded dough, and roll it out again. Fold it again and let stand for about 10 minutes. § Repeat this operation 3 times, letting the dough rest each time for 10 minutes. § Roll out to 3 mm (⅛ in) thickness and use as indicated.

Right:
Preparing plain pastry

Brodo vegetale
Vegetable broth

Makes about 1½ litres (2½ pints); Preparation: 10 minutes; Cooking: 45 minutes; Level of difficulty: Simple
Put all the ingredients in a large pot with about 2 litres (3½ pints) of cold water. Bring to a boil, cover, and simmer over low heat for 45 minutes. § When almost cooked, taste to check there is enough salt. § Mash the vegetables into the broth and strain out any skins or lumps. § Use as indicated in the recipes. If you have any left over, serve as a nourishing, low-calorie consommé with a dash of extra-virgin olive oil and a sprinkling of freshly grated parmesan cheese.

■ INGREDIENTS

- 1 large potato, peeled and chopped
- 2 courgettes (zucchini), 2 carrots, 1 medium leek, cut in thick wheels
- 2 stalks celery, chopped
- 1 medium onion
- 1 medium red tomato
- 5 sprigs parsley
- 10 fresh basil leaves
- 1 teaspoon salt

Brodo di carne
Meat broth

Since broth is used in many dishes and is fairly time-consuming to make, it is best to prepare a large quantity in advance and keep it in the freezer. Freeze it in small quantities so that you can use it as you need it.

Makes about 2½ litres (4¼ pints); Preparation: 10 minutes; Cooking: 1¼ hours; Level of difficulty: Simple
Place the vegetables, meat, bones and salt in a large pot and cover with about 3 litres (5 pints) of cold water. § Bring to a boil over high heat. Partially cover, lower heat and simmer for about an hour. § Remove the bones, meat and vegetables and leave the broth to cool. § When the broth is cool, scoop off and discard any extra fat that forms on the top. Use the broth as indicated in the recipes. § The boiled beef can be eaten hot (it is delicious with *salsa verde* or mustard) or cold in a salad. The vegetables can either be mashed into the broth or served hot or cold with the beef.

■ INGREDIENTS

- 1 large carrot
- 1 medium onion
- 1 large stalk celery
- 4 small tomatoes
- 5 sprigs parsley
- 10 fresh basil leaves
- 1 kg (2 lb) lean boiling beef
- 1 kg (2 lb) marrow bones
- ½ tablespoon salt

Pastella per friggere
Batter

Serves 4; Preparation: 45 minutes; Level of difficulty: Simple
Sift the flour into a bowl, make a hole at the centre and add the egg yolk. § Add the oil and salt and stir in the water a little at a time to obtain a thick but fluid batter without lumps. Set aside for 30-40 minutes. § Just before frying, stir the batter well, add the stiffly beaten egg white and fold in gently.

VARIATIONS
– For a softer batter, use milk instead of water.
– For a puffier and crisper batter, use beer instead of water.

■ INGREDIENTS

- 100 g (3½ oz) plain flour
- 1 egg, separated
- 1 tablespoon extra-virgin olive oil
- pinch of salt
- cold water

Right: *Brodo di carne*

CRÊPES
Crêpes

Delicious crêpes! Make a double batch and serve them as a dessert with lemon juice and sugar, jam, mashed strawberries and cream, flambé (with brandy); the list of mouthwatering possibilities is almost endless.

Makes about 12 Crêpes; Preparation: 1 hour; Cooking: 15 minutes; Level of difficulty: Medium

Beat the eggs in a bowl with a fork or whisk. § Sift the flour and salt into another bowl and stir the milk in gradually, making sure that no lumps form. § When the mixture is smooth, pour it into the eggs. § Beat vigorously for 2-3 minutes, then cover the bowl with plastic wrap and place in the coldest part of the refrigerator for 40-50 minutes. § Before using, beat again for a few seconds. § Set the crêpe pan over medium heat, skewer a piece of butter on the end of a fork and run it around the bottom of the pan until it is well greased. § Using a small ladle, pour 1-2 scoops of batter into the pan. Take the pan off the heat and rotate it so that the batter covers the bottom evenly. § Put it back on the heat and when the crêpe has set, turn it over using a spatula, your hands, or by flipping it. § When golden on both sides, slide it onto a plate. § Keep making crêpes until you run out of batter. Remember to grease the pan for each new crêpe.

■ INGREDIENTS

- 3 eggs
- 80 g (3 oz) plain flour
- pinch of salt
- 350 ml (12fl oz) milk
- 50 g (1½ oz) butter to grease the crêpe pan
- a nonstick pan about 15 cm (6 in) in diameter

SALSA BESCIAMELLA
Béchamel sauce

Béchamel is a basic ingredient in many baked vegetable dishes. Always make a generous amount when using the sauce with vegetables because it is difficult to predict how much they will absorb. If you make too much, use it to revive leftover vegetables (or pasta) by combining them with the béchamel in an ovenproof dish (with a little tomato sauce, if you have it). Sprinkle with freshly grated parmesan and bake for 15 minutes in a hot oven.

Serves 4; Preparation: 5 minutes; Cooking: 10 minutes; Level of difficulty: Simple

Heat the milk in a saucepan until it is almost boiling. § In a heavy-bottomed saucepan, melt the butter with the flour over low heat, stirring rapidly with a wooden spoon. Cook for about 1 minute. § Remove from heat and add half the hot milk, stirring constantly. Return to low heat and stir until the sauce starts to thicken. § Add the rest of the milk gradually and continue stirring until it comes to a boil. § Season with salt to taste and continue stirring until the béchamel is the right thickness. § If any lumps form, beat the sauce rapidly with a fork or whisk until they dissolve.

■ INGREDIENTS

- 500 ml (16fl oz) milk
- 60 g (2 oz) butter
- 60 g (2 oz) plain flour
- salt

Right:
Preparing crêpes

Salsa maionese
Mayonnaise

Making mayonnaise is not easy at first, but with a little patience you will master the art. Homemade mayonnaise is so much better than the store-bought variety, so it really is worth the effort. The best results are achieved by hand, but I have also included instructions for making it in a blender.

■ INGREDIENTS

• 1 fresh egg yolk
• pinch of salt
• 150 ml (5fl oz) extra-virgin olive oil
• freshly ground black pepper
• 1 tablespoon lemon juice (or white vinegar)

Serves 4; Preparation: 15-20 minutes; Level of difficulty: Medium

BY HAND: use a fork, wooden spoon, or hand whisk to beat the egg yolk in a bowl with the salt. § Add the oil a drop at a time at first, then in a steady drizzle, stirring all the time in the same direction. § When the mayonnaise begins to thicken, add, very gradually, the lemon juice (or vinegar), the pepper and a few more drops of oil until it is the right density. § If the mayonnaise curdles, all is not lost. Just start over again with another egg yolk and use the curdled mayonnaise in place of the oil.

IN THE BLENDER: use the same ingredients as above, except for the egg, which should be whole. § Place the egg, salt, pepper, 1-2 tablespoons of oil and the lemon juice (or vinegar) in the blender and blend for a few seconds at maximum speed. § When the ingredients are well mixed, pour the remaining oil into the mixture very gradually. Continue blending until the right density is reached.

Salsa vinaigrette
Vinaigrette (Salad dressing)

■ INGREDIENTS

• 1 tablespoon vinegar
• pinch of salt
• 3 tablespoons extra-virgin olive oil
• 3 pinches freshly ground black pepper

Serves 4; Preparation: 10 minutes; Level of difficulty: Simple

Put the vinegar in a bowl and dissolve the salt in it. § Add the oil and pepper and beat with a whisk or fork to emulsify.

VARIATIONS
– Vary the basic vinaigrette salad dressing by adding other ingredients to taste; for example, finely chopped garlic; onion; spring onions; crispy-fried diced panetta; fresh raw egg yolk; or anchovy paste (in this case leave out the salt) with chopped hard-boiled egg and a clove of finely chopped garlic.
– Add another tablespoon of oil and 100 g (3½ oz) of crumbled gorgonzola cheese to the basic mixture. Mix well to obtain a creamy sauce.
– Add a teaspoon of mild or strong mustard (whichever you prefer) to the basic dressing, or a teaspoon of mustard seeds. Marinate for at least 30 minutes before serving.
– Adding aromatic herbs to the basic dressing is the easiest way to flavour it. Some favourite herbs are: mint, thyme, oregano, chives or chervil.

Right:
Homemade mayonnaise

Braised and Sautéed Vegetables

Almost all vegetables can be braised or sautéed. The idea is to exalt the flavours of the main ingredient without overwhelming it. The authentic recipes in this chapter are only a tiny portion of the full Italian repertoire. Once you have mastered these, use your imagination and personal tastes to invent others.

Zucchine intere ripiene
Stuffed courgettes

If there is any leftover filling, roll it into walnut-sized balls, flour lightly and fry until golden brown. Serve with the filled courgettes.

Serves 4; Preparation: 30-40 minutes; Cooking: 40 minutes; Level of difficulty: Simple

Cut the courgettes in half, remove the pulp and set it aside. § Mix the pork, sausage, mortadella, parmesan, parsley, garlic, eggs, salt and pepper in a bowl. Use a fork to blend the mixture thoroughly. § Stuff the hollowed-out courgettes with the filling. § Heat the frying oil in a sauté pan and cook the stuffed courgette halves for 2-3 minutes. Remove from the oil, and place on paper towels to drain. § To make the sauce, pour the olive oil and tomatoes into a large sauté pan, add 5 tablespoons of courgette pulp, basil and salt and pepper to taste. Cook over medium heat for 5 minutes. § Place the stuffed courgettes in the pan with the sauce and add 1 cup of water. Cook for 20 minutes covered with a sheet of foil with a small hole in it for the steam to escape. Uncover, and cook for 10 minutes more, or until the sauce has reduced. § Serve hot on a bed of parmesan or saffron risotto.

> VARIATION
> – For a spicier filling, use provolone cheese instead of parmesan and finely chopped prosciutto instead of mortadella.

■ INGREDIENTS

- 8 large courgettes (zucchini)
- 250 g (8 oz) minced pork
- 1 Italian pork sausage, skinned and crumbled
- 100 g (3½ oz) mortadella (or ham), coarsely chopped
- 60 g (2 oz) freshly grated parmesan cheese
- 2 tablespoons parsley, 3 cloves garlic, finely chopped together
- 2 beaten eggs
- salt and freshly ground black pepper
- 6 tablespoons oil, for frying
- 4 tablespoons extra-virgin olive oil
- 800 g (1½ lb) peeled and chopped fresh or tinned tomatoes
- 6 basil leaves, torn

Wine: a dry red (Barbera d'Asti)

Zucchine trifolate
Braised courgettes

Serves 4: Preparation: 10 minutes; Cooking: 15 minutes; Level of difficulty: Simple

Cut the cloves of garlic in two and place them in a sauté pan with the oil. Sauté over medium heat until the garlic turns light gold. § Remove the garlic, add the butter and courgettes, and cook over high heat for 5 minutes. § Reduce heat to medium-low, cover, and simmer for 5 more minutes. § Season with salt and pepper, uncover and complete cooking. Don't let the courgettes turn mushy; the wheels should stay whole. § Remove from heat, add the parsley, toss well and transfer to a heated serving dish.

> VARIATIONS
> – Replace the parsley with 1 tablespoon of finely chopped fresh calamint, mint, or tarragon.
> – Add a finely chopped onion and 4 chopped cherry tomatoes.

■ INGREDIENTS

- 2 cloves garlic
- 2 tablespoons extra-virgin olive oil
- 2 tablespoons butter
- 800 g (1¾ lb) small courgettes (zucchini), cut into wheels
- salt and freshly ground black pepper
- 3 tablespoons finely chopped parsley

Wine: a dry red (Chianti)

Right: *Zucchini trifolate*

Peperoni ripieni in tegame
Stuffed peppers

Serves 4; Preparation: 20 minutes; Cooking: 35 minutes; Level of difficulty: Simple

Trim the stalks of the peppers to about 2.5 cm (1 in). Cut their tops off about 2.5 cm (1 in) from the top and set aside. Remove the seeds and membranes. § Soak the bread in cold water for 10 minutes. Squeeze out excess moisture, crumble, and place in a bowl. Season with salt and pepper. § Add the capers, olives, garlic, parsley, basil, anchovies, tomatoes, parmesan and provolone. Add the vinegar and half the oil and mix thoroughly. § Stuff the peppers with the filling, replace the tops, and stand them upright in a pan that is at least as tall as they are. Add the remaining oil and ½ cup of water. § Partially cover the pan and cook over medium-high heat. § Baste the peppers with liquid from the bottom of the pan from time to time. § After about 20 minutes pierce a pepper with the point of a sharp knife; if it penetrates easily, remove the lid and let some of the moisture evaporate. When done, the peppers will be soft and well-cooked. § Serve hot. The delicious dark stock can be poured over the peppers or served separately. § This dish makes a perfect light lunch.

■ INGREDIENTS

- 4 red or yellow peppers
- 8 slices dry bread
- salt and freshly ground black pepper
- 200 g (6½ oz) capers
- 300 g (10 oz) pitted and chopped black olives
- 3 cloves garlic, 3 tablespoons parsley, finely chopped
- 12 fresh basil leaves, torn
- 8 anchovy fillets, crumbled
- 350 g (12 oz) peeled and chopped fresh or tinned tomatoes
- 250 g (8 oz) freshly grated parmesan cheese
- 150 g (5 oz) freshly grated provolone cheese
- 8 tablespoons extra-virgin olive oil
- 1 tablespoon wine vinegar

Wine: a dry red (Chianti Classico)

Fiori e zucchine all'olio
Potatoes and courgettes with courgette flowers

An eyecatching and distinctly southern Italian dish, from the Campania region around Naples. The original recipe calls for fresh chillies; add 2 for a mild dish and 4 for a spicy dish. If you can't get fresh chillies, use the crushed dried variety. Add the chillies together with the courgettes.

Serves 4; Preparation: 15 minutes; Cooking: 25 minutes; Level of difficulty: simple

Sauté the garlic with the oil in a sauté pan until gold. § Add the potatoes, cover, and simmer for 15 minutes, stirring frequently. § Add the courgettes and season with salt, pepper and parsley. Simmer, partially covered, for 5 minutes more. If the vegetables are too watery, remove the lid and let some of the moisture evaporate. § Trim the stems of the courgette flowers just below the bloom, wash carefully, and pat dry with paper towels. § Add 15 flowers to the courgettes and potatoes and cook for 5 minutes more, or until the vegetables are soft but not mushy. § Transfer to a heated serving dish, garnish with the remaining courgette blossoms and serve piping hot.

■ INGREDIENTS

- 2 cloves garlic, finely chopped
- 4 tablespoons extra-virgin olive oil
- 12 small new potatoes
- 8 medium courgettes, cut in thick wheels
- salt and freshly ground black pepper
- 2 tablespoons finely chopped parsley
- 20 courgette flowers

Wine: a dry rosé (Ravello)

Right:
Fagioli all'uccelletto

INGREDIENTS

- 4 cloves garlic, crushed
- 6 tablespoons extra-virgin olive oil
- 400 g (14 oz) peeled and chopped tinned tomatoes
- 8 leaves fresh sage
- salt and freshly ground black pepper
- 400 g (14 oz) white kidney beans, canned, or soaked and pre-cooked

Wine: a dry red (Chianti Classico)

FAGIOLI ALL'UCCELLETTO
Tuscan-style kidney beans

An old Florentine favourite. Delicious when cooked in an earthenware pot. For a spicier dish, add ½ teaspoon crushed chillies. In Tuscany, the dish is traditionally served with Italian pork sausages.

Serves 4; Preparation: 10 minutes; Cooking: 25 minutes; Level of difficulty: Simple

Sauté the garlic in the oil and as soon as it turns light gold, add the tomatoes, sage, salt and pepper. § Simmer over medium heat for 10 minutes. § As the sauce starts to thicken, add the beans and cook for about 15 more minutes. § Serve hot directly from the pot.

Peperoni Vivaci
Mixed peppers with garlic and capers

■ INGREDIENTS
- 1 yellow, 1 green, 2 red medium peppers
- 3 cloves garlic, finely chopped
- 4 tablespoons extra-virgin olive oil
- salt
- 80 ml (3fl oz) vinegar
- 2 tablespoons capers

Wine: a young dry red
(Chianti novello)

Serves 4; Preparation: 15 minutes; Cooking: 20-25 minutes; Level of difficulty: Simple

Cut the peppers lengthwise into 12 mm (½-in) strips. § Sauté the garlic with the oil in a large sauté pan. Add the peppers and press them down with the lid. Season with salt. § Cook over medium heat for about 15 minutes, or until the strips start to wilt. Stir from time to time with a wooden fork. § When the peppers are tender (not mushy), turn the heat up to high and pour the vinegar and capers over the top. Mix rapidly, and cook for 2-3 minutes more to let the vinegar evaporate. § Traditionally served hot or cold as a side dish with meat, *Peperoni vivaci* makes a tempting appetiser when served on toasted slices of wholewheat bread.

VARIATION
– Add 4 crumbled anchovy fillets with the vinegar and capers. In this case, use less salt.

Peperonata
Mixed peppers

■ INGREDIENTS
- 4 peppers, mixed red, yellow and green, cut in 12 mm (½-in) strips
- 3 onions, thickly sliced
- 500 g (1 lb) peeled and chopped fresh or tinned tomatoes
- 3 medium potatoes, cut in 2.5 cm (1 in) squares
- 5 tablespoons extra-virgin olive oil
- 3 cloves garlic, finely chopped
- 8 fresh basil leaves, torn
- salt and freshly ground black pepper

Wine: a dry red
(Sangiovese di Romagna)

Right: *Peperoni vivaci*

One of the classic Italian vegetable dishes.
It is particularly tasty when cooked in an earthenware pot.

Serves 4; Preparation: 20 minutes; Cooking: 30 minutes; Level of difficulty: Simple

Place the vegetables in a large heavy-bottomed saucepan or earthenware pot. Add the oil, garlic, basil, salt and pepper. Cover and cook over medium heat. § After 15 minutes turn the heat up to medium-high and partially uncover to let some of the liquid from the peppers evaporate. § As the dish cooks, the potatoes will soften, absorbing the flavours of the other vegetables. § Traditionally served hot or cold as a side dish with grilled or roasted meats, *Peperonata* has enough character to be served as a main course with rice, couscous or baked potatoes.

VARIATION
– For a stronger, more distinctive flavour, add a medium aubergine (eggplant), diced but not peeled, black olives, and a sprinkling of oregano.

■ INGREDIENTS

- 2 medium onions, cut in medium-thick slices
- 2 large cloves garlic, finely chopped
- 4 medium carrots, cut in wheels and crescents
- 500 g (1 lb) peeled and chopped fresh or tinned tomatoes
- 8 leaves fresh basil
- 600 g (1¼ lb) green beans
- 4 tablespoons extra-virgin olive oil
- salt and freshly ground black pepper

Wine: a dry red
(Dolcetto d'Alba)

Fagiolini in umido con carote
Green beans and carrots cooked with onions, garlic and tomatoes

Serves 4; Preparation: 15 minutes; Cooking: 30 minutes; Level of difficulty: Simple

Put all the ingredients in a large heavy-bottomed saucepan (or earthenware pot). Season with salt and pepper. § Cover and cook for 20 minutes over medium heat, stirring frequently. At first the beans will stay on top until the steam softens them and you can mix them in. § Uncover the pan and continue cooking until the sauce has reduced sufficiently and the beans are crunchy but cooked. § Serve hot or cold as a side dish with grilled, braised or sautéed meats, or as a light lunch with rice, potatoes or lots of crunchy fresh bread.

VARIATION
– Add two large stalks of diced celery.

■ INGREDIENTS

- 800 g (1¾ lb) white baby onions, peeled
- 2 tablespoons extra-virgin olive oil
- 3 tablespoons butter
- salt and freshly ground black pepper
- 500 ml (16fl oz) white wine
- 3 whole bay leaves

Wine: a dry white
(Galestro)

Cipolline brasate al vino
White baby onions braised in white wine

Serves 4; Preparation: 10 minutes; Cooking: 30 minutes; Level of difficulty: Simple

Place the onions, oil and butter in a heavy-bottomed sauté pan. § Sauté over high heat for about 10 minutes, stirring the onions with a wooden spoon so that they brown evenly. Season with salt and pepper. § Add the wine and bay leaves, partially cover, and cook for 15 more minutes. § Uncover and let the sauce thicken. § Serve hot or at room temperature with any kind of roast meat or fish.

VARIATIONS
– Add a tablespoon of tomato paste with the wine, to make the onions pink.
– For a sweeter, more aromatic dish, soak 2 tablespoons of raisins in the wine. Add the raisins and a bouquet of herbs (thyme, marjoram, mint) together with the bay leaves.

Left:
Fagiolini in umido con carote

Melanzane al Funghetto
Aubergine cooked in tomato and garlic

This dish also makes an excellent pasta sauce. For 4 people, add 3 extra tomatoes and another tablespoon of oil to the ingredients listed here. Serve over 450 g (14 oz) of any sort of dried short pasta (penne, conchiglie, fusilli, maccheroni) cooked in salted, boiling water until al dente.

Serves 4; Preparation: 15 minutes; Cooking: 30 minutes; Level of difficulty: Simple

Trim the ends off the aubergines and cut them in quarters lengthwise. Slice the quarters into pieces about 5 cm (2 in) long. § Sauté the garlic with the oil in a large sauté pan until it turns gold. § Add the aubergines, season with salt and pepper, stir well and cover. Cook over medium-low heat for 15 minutes. § Add the tomatoes, mix well, and cook for 10 more minutes over medium heat. § For the last 5 minutes, remove the lid and add the parsley. § Serve hot as a pasta sauce, or as a side dish with any sort of roast or fried meat or fish.

■ INGREDIENTS

- 6 long aubergines (eggplants)
- 4 cloves garlic, finely chopped
- 3 tablespoons extra-virgin olive oil
- salt and freshly ground black pepper
- 3 medium tomatoes, peeled and diced
- 2 tablespoons finely chopped parsley

Wine: a dry red (Valpolicella)

Melanzane a Librino
Filled aubergine "sandwiches"

Serves 4; Preparation: 2¼ hours; Cooking: 30 minutes; Level of difficulty: Medium

Using a sharp knife, cut each aubergine in three crosswise. Slice each piece down the middle, leaving it attached on one side, and open it out like a book. § Place the aubergines in layers in a large dish and sprinkle with salt. Cover with a plate with a heavy weight on top to press the bitter liquid out of the aubergine. Leave to drain for 2 hours. § Put the beaten eggs in a bowl, add the pork, parsley, garlic and parmesan. Blend well with a fork for 2-3 minutes. § Put the aubergine in a colander and rinse well under cold running water to remove all the salt. Squeeze the moisture out gently with your hands and pat dry with paper towels. § Using a teaspoon, stuff the pieces of aubergine with the filling so that they look like plump little sandwiches. § Heat the frying oil in a frying pan and dip the aubergine sandwiches in one by one, turning them with two forks to seal the edges so that the filling stays inside. § Place on paper towels to eliminate excess oil. § To prepare the sauce, heat the olive oil in a sauté pan and add the tomatoes and basil. Cook over medium-low heat for 15 minutes. Season with salt and pepper. § Add the aubergine sandwiches and cover with sauce. Simmer over low heat for 5 minutes, or until the sauce begins to reduce. § Serve hot with a green salad as a main course.

■ INGREDIENTS

- 8 long aubergines (eggplants)
- salt
- 4 eggs, beaten
- 500 g (1 lb) minced pork
- 2 tablespoons finely chopped parsley
- 3 cloves garlic, finely chopped
- 100 g (3½ oz) freshly grated parmesan cheese
- oil for frying
- 700 g (1¼ lb) peeled and chopped tinned tomatoes
- 6 fresh basil leaves
- 4 tablespoons extra-virgin olive oil
- freshly ground black pepper

Wine: a dry red (Brindisi Riserva)

Right:
Melanzane al funghetto

Carciofi Ritti
Roman-style stuffed braised artichokes

This dish is also known as "Carciofi alla Romana" because it come from Lazio, the region around Rome.

Serves 4; Preparation: 30 minutes; Cooking: 25-30 minutes; Level of difficulty: Simple

Prepare the artichokes as shown on p. 8. Cut the stems short and place them in a bowl of cold water with the lemon juice. Set aside for 10 minutes. § Put the artichokes and 2 tablespoons of oil in a sauté pan with sides high enough to cook the artichokes in an upright position. § Open the leaves carefully and stuff them by placing a spoonful of garlic and parsley (leave 2 spoonfuls for garnishing), pieces of pancetta, flakes of pecorino and a spoonful of parmesan in each artichoke. Press the filling down and close the leaves. § Sprinkle the stuffed artichokes with the remaining garlic and parsley and pour the wine and remaining oil over the top. Season with salt (not too much — the pancetta and pecorino are both salty) and pepper. § Cover with foil, leaving a small opening for steam to escape, and cook over medium heat. § Baste the artichokes with their sauce from time to time. § When the sauce has reduced to about 2.5 cm (1 in) in the bottom of the pan, the artichokes are ready. § Serve hot as a light lunch or side dish with roast or grilled meat.

> VARIATION
> – The artichokes can also be filled as follows: crumble about 200 g (7 oz) of mozzarella cheese in a bowl with 2 tablespoons of finely chopped parsley, 3 tablespoons of bread crumbs, 3 tablespoons of freshly grated parmesan cheese, and 2 beaten eggs. Season with salt and pepper, mix well, and stuff the artichokes. Cook with wine and oil as above. This recipe gives the artichokes a more delicate flavour.

■ INGREDIENTS

• 8 large artichokes
• juice of 1 lemon
• 5 tablespoons extra-virgin olive oil
• 4 cloves garlic, 4 tablespoons parsley, finely chopped together
• 250 g (8 oz) pancetta, diced
• 150 g (5 oz) pecorino romano cheese, in flakes
• 8 tablespoons freshly grated parmesan cheese
• 300 ml (10fl oz) dry white wine
• salt and freshly ground black pepper

Wine: a dry rosé
(Lagrein Rosato)

Spezzatino di Carciofi
Artichoke stew

Serves 4; Preparation: 20 minutes; Cooking: 25 minutes; Level of difficulty: Simple

Prepare the artichokes as shown on p. 8. Remove all but the tender, white inner leaves. Peel the stems and cut them into wheels. § Put the artichokes and stems in a bowl of cold water with the lemon juice. Set aside for 10 minutes. § Drain the artichokes and cut them into quarters. § Place the artichoke quarters and stems, garlic, oil, wine, salt and pepper in a heavy-

■ INGREDIENTS

• 8 medium artichokes
• juice of 1 lemon
• 3 cloves garlic, finely chopped
• 4 tablespoons extra-virgin olive oil
• 250 ml (8fl oz) dry white wine

Right:
Spezzatino di carciofi

- salt and freshly ground
  black pepper
- 3 tablespoons parsley,
  finely chopped

Wine: a dry white
(Greco di Tufo)

bottomed pan. Cook for 20 minutes covered, then uncover and add the parsley; stir and finish cooking without a lid. § Serve hot at lunch with a platter of fresh, light cheeses (mozzarella, ricotta, caprino), or as a side dish with liver braised in butter and sage, or with oven-roasted or braised meats.

VARIATION
– Replace the parsley with mint or thyme and add 1½ tablespoons of tomato paste to the cooking liquid.

Mamme di Carciofi Ripiene
Stuffed artichokes

■ INGREDIENTS

• 8 large artichokes
• juice of 1 lemon
• 4 eggs, beaten
• salt and black pepper
• 150 g (5 oz) minced pork
• 1 Italian pork sausage, skinned and crumbled
• 150 g (5 oz) prosciutto, chopped
• 150 g (5 oz) freshly grated parmesan cheese
• 3 cloves garlic, 2 tablespoons parsley, finely chopped
• 250 ml (8fl oz) oil, for frying
• 8 tablespoons extra-virgin olive oil
• 800 g (1½ lb) peeled and chopped tinned tomatoes
• 10 fresh basil leaves, torn
Wine: a dry red (Chianti)

Serves 4; Preparation: 25 minutes; Cooking: 1 hour; Level of difficulty: Medium

Clean the artichokes as shown on p. 8. Trim the stems short so that the artichokes will stand upright in the pot. Chop the stems coarsely and soak them with the artichokes in a bowl of cold water and lemon juice for 10 minutes. § Season the beaten eggs with salt and pepper and add the pork, sausage, prosciutto, parmesan, garlic and parsley. Blend well with a fork. § Using a teaspoon, fill the heart of each artichoke. § Heat the frying oil in a frying pan and when it is hot enough hold each artichoke upside down in the oil for about 2 minutes, to seal in the filling. Roll the artichokes in the oil for 2 more minutes to cook the leaves. Using two forks, remove from the oil and set aside. § Place the olive oil, tomatoes, basil, artichoke stems, salt and pepper in a sauté pan and simmer over medium heat for 10 minutes. § Add the stuffed artichokes and baste them with the sauce. Cover and simmer for 20 minutes. Uncover and cook for 10 more minutes, or until the sauce has reduced. § Serve hot as a main course.

Tortino di Carciofi
Florentine artichoke omelette

■ INGREDIENTS

• 5 large artichokes
• juice of 1 lemon
• 4 tablespoons extra-virgin olive oil
• 5 eggs
• 125 ml (4fl oz) water
• salt and freshly ground black pepper

Wine: a dry red (Sassicaia)

A classic Florentine recipe, as old as the city itself. A real Florentine artichoke omelette should be slightly underdone; the eggs should be cooked underneath and moist on top.

Serves 4; Preparation: 20 minutes; Cooking: 25-30 minutes; Level of difficulty: Simple

Clean the artichokes as shown on p. 8. Cut the stems short. Soak the artichokes in a bowl of cold water and lemon juice for 10 minutes. § Cut the artichokes into 2.5 cm (½-in) slices and place in a large sauté pan with the oil. Add the water and salt to taste, cover and cook for 7-8 minutes. § Uncover and continue cooking until the artichokes are soft and golden brown and the water has evaporated. § Beat the eggs with salt and pepper until foamy and pour over the artichokes. Cover and cook for 5 minutes over medium heat. Uncover and continue cooking. As the eggs begin to set, puncture them with a fork to release the liquid part and help it cook. § Serve hot with a large green salad seasoned with garlic, oil and vinegar.

Right:
Tortino di carciofi

■ INGREDIENTS

• 3 heads escarole

• 4 tablespoons extra-
  virgin olive oil

• 50 g (2 oz) pine nuts

• 50 g (2 oz) raisins soaked
  for 30 minutes in water

• 12 pitted and chopped
  black olives

• salt and freshly ground
  black pepper

• 40 g (1½ oz) capers

• 4 anchovy fillets, finely
  chopped or 3 curls of
  anchovy paste

*Wine: a dry white
(Pinot Grigio)*

INDIVIA SCAROLA DOLCE FORTE DELICATA
Escarole with pine nuts, capers, olives, raisins and anchovies

Serves 4; Preparation: 15 minutes; Cooking: 20 minutes; Level of difficulty: Simple

Use the green leaves of the escarole and set the creamy white hearts aside to use in a salad. § Blanch the leaves in salted, boiling water, drain well, and spread in a colander to dry for about 10 minutes. § Place the oil in a sauté pan and add the escarole, pine nuts, raisins, olives, salt and pepper. Sauté over medium heat for 10 minutes. Use a fork and spoon to toss the leaves from time to time as they cook. § Add the capers and anchovy, toss well and cook until any excess water has evaporated. § Serve hot as a first course, or as a side dish with grilled or roast meat – the earthy flavour is perfect with all white and red meats.

■ INGREDIENTS

• 2 large heads celery

• juice of 1 lemon

• salt and freshly ground
  black pepper

• 4 tablespoons extra-
  virgin olive oil

• 1 large potato, diced

• 60 g (2 oz) pancetta,
  diced

• 1 cup fresh cream

*Wine: a young dry red
(Vino Novello)*

CUORI DI SEDANO DELICATI
Celery hearts in cream sauce with pancetta and potato

Serves 4; Preparation: 5 minutes; Cooking: 30 minutes; Level of difficulty: Simple

Remove the tough outer stalks of celery and cut the ends off level with the hearts. Divide the inner stalks in half lengthwise. § Put the lemon juice in a pot of salted water and bring to a boil. Cook the celery for 7-8 minutes. Drain well and place on a serving dish. § Place the oil in a frying pan and fry the potato. § Remove most of the oil, add the pancetta and cook until crisp. § Heat the cream in a saucepan over low heat with salt and pepper to taste. Cook until it thickens. § Pour the cream over the celery hearts and sprinkle the potatoes and pancetta on top. § Serve hot as an appetiser or as side dish with grilled fish or braised white meats.

VARIATION
– For a tastier dish, add 2 tablespoons of grated pecorino romano or provolone cheese to the cream before heating it (or parmesan cheese with a tablespoon of basic tomato sauce – see recipe p. 20).

Left:
Cuori di sedano delicati

Cavolini di Bruxelles alla diavola
Hot and spicy Brussels sprouts

Serves 4-6; Preparation: 10 minutes; Cooking: 25 minutes; Level of difficulty: Simple

Cook the Brussels sprouts in salted, boiling water for 7-8 minutes, drain well and set aside. § In a sauté pan or earthenware pot, sauté the garlic in the oil until golden. § Add the pancetta and sausage. Sauté briefly and stir in the Brussels sprouts and crushed chillies. § Season with salt, cover, and cook for 10 minutes. § Uncover, sprinkle with the chives and cook for 5 more minutes. § Serve piping hot on a bed of rice as a main course.

Cavolini di Bruxelles al curry
Curried Brussels sprouts

Serves 4-6; Preparation: 20 minutes; Cooking: 30 minutes; Level of difficulty: Simple

Sauté the onion in the butter in a large sauté pan until golden. § Add the flour and mix well, stirring rapidly with a wooden spoon. Add half the meat stock a little at a time, stirring constantly. § Add the apple and stir in the remaining stock a little at a time as the sauce simmers over low heat for about 20 minutes. The mixture should boil slowly as the apple disintegrates and blends in with the other ingredients. After 20 minutes the sauce should be thick and creamy. If you want a perfectly smooth sauce, put it through the food mill. § Add the cream and curry powder, season with salt and pepper, and simmer for 5 more minutes, stirring constantly. § In the meantime, cook the sprouts for about 10 minutes in salted, boiling water. Drain well and arrange on a heated serving dish. § Pour the hot sauce over the top and serve immediately as a main course with saffron-flavoured rice, or as a side dish with chicken cooked in a white wine sauce or veal scaloppini braised with onions.

■ INGREDIENTS

- 1 kg (2 lb) Brussels sprouts
- 3 cloves garlic, finely chopped
- 3 tablespoons extra-virgin olive oil
- 100 g (3½ oz) smoked pancetta (or bacon), diced
- 1 Italian sausage, skinned and crumbled
- ½ teaspoon crushed chillies
- salt
- 1 bunch chives, coarsely chopped

Wine: a dry red (Sangiovese)

■ INGREDIENTS

- 1 medium onion, finely chopped
- 2 tablespoons butter
- 1 tablespoon sifted plain flour
- 500 ml (16fl oz) meat stock (see recipe p. 24, or make using a bouillon cube and hot water)
- 1 sweet Golded Delicious apple, peeled and sliced
- 250 ml (8fl oz) fresh cream
- 1½ tablespoons curry powder
- salt and freshly ground black pepper
- 1 kg (2 lb) Brussels sprouts

Wine: a dry white (Bianco di Pitigliano)

Right: *Cavolini di Bruxelles al curry*

Funghi misti in fricassea
Mixed mushrooms in egg sauce

Timing is important in this recipe. The egg sauce must be poured over the mushrooms the moment they are removed from the heat and tossed quickly so that the egg doesn't cook but turns into a creamy sauce.

Serves 4; Preparation: 15 minutes; Cooking: 25 minutes; Level of difficulty: Medium

Cook the onion in a large sauté pan with the oil until transparent. § Slice the larger mushrooms in thick slices and leave the smaller varieties whole. § Add the mushrooms to the sauté pan. Season with salt and pepper, cover, and cook for 15-20 minutes over medium-low heat. Stir frequently. § When the mushrooms are cooked, remove from heat and transfer to a heated serving dish. § While the mushrooms are cooking, beat the egg yolks in a bowl with the lemon juice and parsley until foamy. § Pour the egg sauce over the mushrooms and toss quickly so that the egg doesn't set but becomes a creamy sauce. § Serve with a large green salad and fresh bread as a light lunch.

■ INGREDIENTS

- 1 medium onion, finely chopped
- 4 tablespoons extra-virgin olive oil
- 1 kg (2 lb) mixed fresh or frozen mushrooms (porcini, white, chanterelle, or Caesar's), washed and trimmed
- salt and freshly ground black pepper
- 4 egg yolks
- juice of 1 lemon
- 2 tablespoons finely chopped parsley

Wine: a young dry red (Novello Falo')

Funghi porcini trifolati
Stewed porcini mushrooms

The traditional Italian recipe calls for fresh porcini mushrooms which are hard to find outside Italy or France. If you can't get porcini mushrooms, replace them with the same quantity of fresh shiitake mushrooms, or with 1¾ pounds of white mushrooms and ¼ cup of dried porcini mushrooms soaked in a bowl of cold water for 20 minutes.

Serves 4-6; Preparation: 15 minutes; Cooking: 15 minutes; Level of difficulty: Simple

Trim the stalks off the mushrooms and separate the heads from the stems. § Cut the stems in half lengthwise. Chop the stems and heads in thick slices. § Sauté the garlic in a large sauté pan until golden. Add the stems and sauté for 7-8 minutes. § Add the mushroom heads, salt and pepper and stir carefully with a wooden spoon. § Add the calamint and finish cooking over low heat. § Serve hot as an appetiser on squares of toasted wholewheat bread or as a side dish with braised meat.

■ INGREDIENTS

- 1 kg (2 lb) fresh porcini mushrooms
- 3 large cloves garlic, finely chopped
- 4 tablespoons extra-virgin olive oil
- salt and freshly ground black pepper
- 1 tablespoon of fresh or ½ tablespoon dried calamint or thyme

Wine: a dry red (Brunello di Montalcino)

VARIATION
– Replace the porcini with chanterelle mushrooms and add 3 cherry tomatoes (cut in half and squashed with a fork) halfway through cooking.

Right:
Funghi porcini trifolati

■ INGREDIENTS

- 750 g (1½ lb) fresh or frozen white mushrooms
- 2 medium potatoes, diced
- 5 tablespoons extra-virgin olive oil
- 3 cloves garlic, crushed
- salt and freshly ground black pepper
- 100 g (3½ oz) pine nuts
- 60 g (2 oz) almond shavings
- 1 bunch calamint

Wine: a dry red (Teroldego)

FUNGHETTI E PATATINE AI PINOLI
Mushrooms and potatoes with pine nuts

Serves 4; Preparation: 10 minutes; Cooking: 25 minutes; Level of difficulty: Simple

Chop any larger mushrooms in thick slices and leave the smaller ones whole. § Cook the potatoes with the oil and garlic in a large sauté pan. § Add the mushrooms and sauté. Season with salt and pepper, cover, and cook for 5 minutes. § Uncover and let some of the moisture evaporate. Stir in the pine nuts and almonds and cook for 10 more minutes. § Sprinkle with calamint just before removing from heat. § Serve hot with rice and a green salad at lunch.

Pisellini primavera al prezzemolo e prosciutto
Spring peas with prosciutto and parsley

■ INGREDIENTS

- 1.5 kg (3 lb) unshelled or 750 g (1½ lb) frozen peas
- 4 tablespoons extra-virgin olive oil
- 200 g (6½ oz) prosciutto, diced
- 2 large cloves garlic, finely chopped
- water – 400 ml (12 fl oz) for fresh peas, 250 ml (8fl oz) for frozen peas
- 3 tablespoons parsley, finely chopped
- salt and freshly ground black pepper

Wine: a dry red (Chianti Classico)

Serves 4-6; Preparation: 15 minutes; Cooking: 25 minutes; Level of difficulty: Simple

Shell the peas, place them in a colander and rinse under cold running water. § Put the oil in a sauté pan and sauté with the prosciutto. Remove from heat. § Let the oil cool a little, then add the peas, garlic, parsley and water. Partially cover, and simmer for about 15 minutes. § Season with salt and pepper. § Serve hot as a side dish with roast beef or oven-baked fish.

VARIATIONS
– Replace the garlic with 1 medium onion, finely chopped.
– Add a teaspoon of sugar to make the peas sweeter.

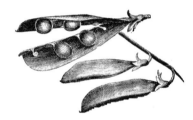

Mousse di piselli
Pea mousse

■ INGREDIENTS

- 1 pound shelled or frozen peas
- 1 medium onion, cut in half
- 450 g (14 oz) ricotta cheese
- 3 tablespoons extra-virgin olive oil
- salt and freshly ground black pepper
- 1 carrot, cut in thin wheels
- 8 tiny sprigs parsley

Wine: a dry red (Oltrepò Pavese)

Serves 4; Preparation: 2½ hours; Cooking: 15 minutes; Level of difficulty: Simple

Bring 2 litres (3½ pints) of salted water to a boil in a pan and cook the peas and onion for 10-15 minutes. § Drain well and set aside to cool. § Place the ricotta, peas, onion and oil in a blender and blend until the mixture is creamy. Season with salt and pepper. § Line a pudding mould of about 1-litre (1¾ pint) capacity with plastic wrap and pour the mixture in, pressing with a spoon to eliminate any air bubbles. Knock the mould against the work bench to eliminate air pockets. § Refrigerate for at least 2 hours. § Invert onto a round serving dish and garnish with the carrot wheels and sprigs of parsley. § Serve on slices of wholewheat toast as an appetiser or as a side dish with braised or grilled fish.

VARIATION
– For a sharper flavour, replace the ricotta cheese with robiola or caprino cheese and place 300 g (10 oz) of finely chopped lean ham in layers at the centre of the mousse.

Right: *Pisellini primavera al prezzemolo e prosciutto*

Asparagi eleganti
Asparagus with brandy and cream sauce

■ INGREDIENTS

• 1 kg (2 lb) fresh
  asparagus
• salt and freshly ground
  black pepper
• 5 tablespoons butter
• 80 ml (3fl oz) brandy
• 600 ml (19fl oz) fresh
  cream
• 1 tablespoon bread
  crumbs

Wine: a dry white
(Corvo Bianco)

Serves 4; Preparation: 15 minutes; Cooking: 25 minutes; Level of difficulty: Simple

Choose a pan large enough to lay the asparagus flat, fill with cold water, and bring to a boil. Add 1 tablespoon of salt and cook the asparagus for about 7-10 minutes (depending on the thickness of the stalks). § Drain well and cut off the tough white part at the bottom of the stalks. § Melt the butter in a sauté pan and add the asparagus. Season with salt and pepper and cook for 3-4 minutes over medium heat. § Pour in the brandy and let it evaporate. Keep the asparagus moving by shaking the sauté pan gently by the handle. § Meanwhile, put the cream and bread crumbs in a saucepan, mix well and cook over medium heat for 10-15 minutes, or until the sauce is thick and creamy. Stir frequently. § Place the asparagus stalks on a heated serving dish and pour the sauce over the top. § Serve as an appetiser with liver pâté on toasted slices of plain or wholewheat bread.

Cicoria catalogna in padella
Catalonia chicory with garlic and anchovies

■ INGREDIENTS

• 1 large head chicory
• 5 cloves garlic, finely
  chopped
• ½ teaspoon crushed
  chillies
• 5 tablespoons extra-virgin
  olive oil
• salt
• 8 anchovy fillets,
  crumbled
• 60 g (2 oz) capers

Wine: a dry red
(Valpolicella)

Serves 4; Preparation: 10 minutes; Cooking: 30 minutes; Level of difficulty: Simple

Trim the head of chicory, remove any yellow or wilted leaves and divide it in two. Wash in cold running water. § Cook in a pan of salted, boiling water for 10-15 minutes. § Drain thoroughly without squeezing and cut lengthwise into 5 cm (2 in) pieces. § Sauté the garlic with the oil in a large sauté pan until golden. § Add the chicory and chillies, and season with a pinch of salt (not too much – remember the capers and anchovies to be added later). § Cook over medium heat for about 10 minutes, stirring frequently. § Add the anchovies and capers and stir them in over high heat for 2-3 minutes. § Serve on a heated serving dish with beef sautéed in sage and garlic, grilled sausages or mixed roast meats.

Right:
Asparagi eleganti

■ INGREDIENTS

- 1 kg (2 lb) fresh or 750 g (1½ lb) frozen spinach
- 4 large cloves garlic, finely chopped
- 4 tablespoons extra-virgin olive oil
- salt

Wine: a dry white
(Riesling Isonzo)

Spinaci saltati

Spinach sautéed with olive oil and garlic

Serves 6; Preparation: 10 minutes; Cooking: 30 minutes; Level of difficulty: Simple

Cook the spinach in a pot of salted, boiling water until tender (3-4 minutes if frozen, 8-10 minutes if fresh). Drain, cool under cold running water, squeeze out excess moisture, and chop coarsely. § Sauté the garlic in the oil until golden. § Add the spinach and cook over medium-high heat for 3-4 minutes, tossing continually, so that the spinach absorbs the flavours of the garlic and oil. § Serve hot with poached eggs or as a side dish with roast or braised meat dishes.

CARDI AL SUGO DI CARNE E PARMIGIANO
Cardoons in meat sauce with parmesan cheese

A cardoon looks a bit like a large white celery. It is closely related to the artichoke, although it has a much stronger taste. Cardoons are not always easy to find, even in Italy. For a completely different, but equally delicious dish, replace the cardoon with the same amount of celery. In this case, there is no need to soak the celery in lemon juice and cooking time will be reduced to 15-20 minutes.

Serves 4; Preparation: 15 minutes; Cooking: 35 minutes; Level of difficulty: Simple

Prepare the cardoon by removing any damaged outer stalks and tough filaments with a sharp knife. Separate the stalks from the heart and cut them into pieces about 7.5 cm (3 in) long. Wash well and soak in a bowl of cold water with the lemon juice for about 10 minutes. § Bring a pot of salted water to a boil. Add the flour and pieces of cardoon and cook for 20 minutes. Drain well. § Heat the meat sauce with the butter in a large sauté pan with sides at least 2 inches high. Add the cardoon pieces a few at a time and mix well with the sauce. When they are all in the pan, season with salt and pepper. Partially cover and cook over low heat for 10-15 minutes, or until the cardoons are tender. Stir frequently. § When cooked, sprinkle with parmesan and let stand for a minute, covered. § Serve hot at lunch with crunchy fresh bread and a mixed salad.

■ INGREDIENTS

• 1 cardoon, weighing about 1 kg (2 lb)
• juice of 2 lemons
• 1½ tablespoons plain flour
• 60 g (2 oz) butter
• 15 tablespoons meat sauce (see recipe p. 20)
• salt and freshly ground black pepper
• 4 tablespoons freshly grated parmesan cheese

*Wine: a dry red
(Rosso di Montepulciano)*

CAROTE CARAMELLATE AL PREZZEMOLO
Carrots in caramel sauce with parsley

If the sauce reduces too much during cooking, add a little white wine (before adding the parsley).

Serves 6; Preparation: 10 minutes; Cooking: 25 minutes; Level of difficulty: Simple

Peel the carrots with a peeler or scrape them with a knife. Rinse well under cold running water. § Cut the carrots into sticks about 5 cm (2 in) long (if you are using baby carrots, leave them whole). § Place them in a large sauté pan and almost cover with cold water. Add half the butter cut into cubes. § Cook over high heat until the water evaporates. § Season with salt and pepper, add the remaining butter and sprinkle with the sugar. Sauté the carrots until they are all a bright orange colour, shiny and caramel-coated. § Add the parsley, mix well, and serve hot with grilled or roasted fish or red meats.

■ INGREDIENTS

• 1.5 kg (3 lb) carrots
• 50 g (1½ oz) butter
• salt and freshly ground black pepper
• 2 tablespoons castor sugar
• 3 tablespoons finely chopped parsley

*Wine: a dry white
(Orvieto Classico)*

Right:
Carote caramellate al prezzemolo

■ INGREDIENTS

- 1.5 kg (3 lb) broad beans in their pods
- 100 g (3½ oz) pancetta, diced
- 2 tablespoons extra-virgin olive oil
- 1 medium onion, finely chopped
- 250 ml (8fl oz) meat broth – see recipe p. 24, or 1 beef bouillon cube dissolved in 250 ml (8fl oz) boiling water
- salt and freshly ground black pepper

Wine: a dry white
(Vernaccia di San Gimignano)

■ INGREDIENTS

- 300 g (10 oz) lentils, soaked in cold water overnight
- 1 medium onion, 1 large carrot, 2 stalks celery, finely chopped together
- 4 tablespoons extra-virgin olive oil
- 60 g (2 oz) pancetta, diced
- 250 ml (8fl oz) white wine
- 1½ tablespoons tomato paste, diluted in 2 tablespoons hot water
- 1 beef bouillon cube
- salt and freshly ground black pepper
- 5 Italian sausages, pricked with a fork to eliminate excess fat while frying

Wine: a dry red (Merlot)

Left:
Lenticchie stufate con salsiccia

FAVE FRESCHE ALLA PANCETTA
Fresh broad beans with pancetta

Serves 4; Preparation: 15 minutes; Cooking: 30 minutes; Level of difficulty: Simple

Pod the beans and set them aside in a bowl of cold water. § Put the pancetta and onion in a sauté pan with the oil and sauté over medium-low heat until the onion is light gold in colour. § Drain the broad beans and add with the broth to the sauté pan. Season with salt and pepper. § Partially cover, and cook over medium-low heat for about 20 minutes, or until the beans are tender and the broth has reduced. § Serve piping hot.

LENTICCHIE STUFATE CON SALSICCIA
Stewed lentils with Italian sausages

Serves 4; Preparation: 10 minutes; Cooking: 1½ hours; Level of difficulty: Simple

Discard any lentils floating on top of the water. § Put the lentils in a pot and just cover with cold water. Add salt and simmer for 30 minutes, then drain. § Put the onion, carrot, celery and pancetta in a large sauté pan with the oil and sauté until golden brown. § Add the lentils and stir for 2-3 minutes to mix them in well. § Pour in the white wine and let it evaporate a little, then add the diluted tomato paste and the bouillon cube. Season with salt and pepper, and cover with hot water. Cook for 40 minutes over a low heat. § In the meantime, brown the sausages in a sauté pan with 2 tablespoons of cold water. Drain the excess fat and add the sausages to the lentils when they have been cooking for about 20 minutes, so they add their flavour to the dish. § When cooked, the lentils should be tender and the stew slightly liquid; if it is too watery, stir over high heat until it reduces sufficiently. § Serve hot as a hearty and complete main course.

VARIATION
– For a spicier dish, add 1 teaspoon crushed chillies with the tomato paste.

Involtini di verza
Stuffed cabbage rolls

Serves 4; Preparation: 30 minutes; Cooking: 45 minutes; Level of difficulty: Medium

Trim the cabbage, discarding the tough outer leaves. Choose 8 large cabbage leaves, make a small cut in the stem of each, and blanch them in salted, boiling water for 4-5 minutes. Drain well, and lay them to dry on a clean tea towel. § Put the beef, pork, sausages, parmesan, eggs, garlic, parsley, salt and pepper in a bowl and mix well with a fork. § Distribute the filling evenly, placing a part on one half of each leaf. Fold the other half over the top, press down, and tuck in the two remaining open ends. Tie with kitchen string. § Sauté the onion in the butter and oil in a large sauté pan until light gold. § Add the stuffed cabbage leaves. Cook on both sides, turning them carefully with a fork or spoon. § Add the tomatoes, season with salt and pepper and cook over medium-low heat for about 35 minutes. If the sauce gets too dry, correct with the meat broth. § Serve hot as a main course with saffron risotto or plain white rice.

■ INGREDIENTS

- 1 medium cabbage
- 150 g (5 oz) lean beef, 150 g (5 oz) lean pork, minced
- 150 g (5 oz) Italian sausages, skinned and crumbled
- 60 g (2 oz) freshly grated parmesan cheese
- 2 eggs
- 2 cloves garlic, 2 tablespoons parsley, finely chopped
- salt and black pepper
- 2 tablespoons butter
- 3 tablespoons extra-virgin olive oil
- 1 onion, finely chopped
- 600 g (20 oz) tinned tomatoes
- 250 ml (8fl oz) meat broth (see recipe p. 24)

Wine: a dry red (Bonarda)

Involtini di lattuga saporiti
Stuffed lettuce-leaf rolls

Serves 4; Preparation: 30 minutes; Cooking: 40 minutes; Level of difficulty: Medium

Wash the lettuce leaves, taking care not to tear them. § Bring a pot of salted water to a boil and blanch each leaf by dipping it into the water for about 20 seconds. Lay the leaves on a clean tea towel to dry. § Brown the sausages in a sauté pan without oil. Add the wine and let it evaporate. Remove from heat and set to cool on a plate, leaving any fat in the sauté pan. § Beat the eggs in a bowl, add the salt, pepper, edam, parmesan, bread crumbs and sausage. Mix well to make a smooth filling. § Distribute the filling evenly among the lettuce leaves and roll them up, folding in the ends to make packages or rolls. Tie with kitchen string. § Put the onion in a sauté pan with the oil over medium heat and sauté until transparent. § Place the stuffed lettuce leaves in the sauté pan with the onion, cover, and cook for 5 minutes. Turn the lettuce rolls with a fork, uncover and cook for 5 more minutes. § Serve hot as a main course with a mushroom risotto or taglierini al limone.

■ INGREDIENTS

- 8 large lettuce leaves
- 250 g (8 oz) Italian sausages, skinned and crumbled
- 3 tablespoons white wine
- 2 eggs
- salt and freshly ground black pepper
- 100 g (3½ oz) edam cheese, and 100 g (3½ oz) parmesan cheese, freshly grated
- 3 tablespoons bread crumbs
- 4 tablespoons extra-virgin olive oil
- 1 onion, finely chopped

Wine: a dry white (Chardonnay)

Right: *Involtini di verza*

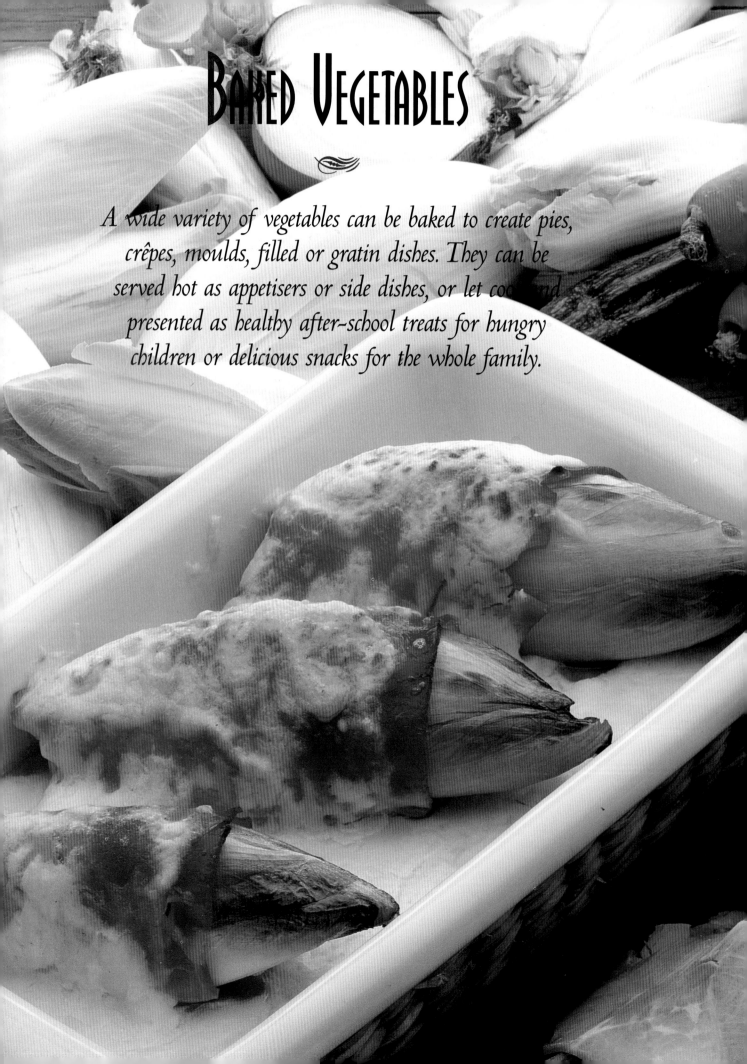

BAKED VEGETABLES

A wide variety of vegetables can be baked to create pies,
crêpes, moulds, filled or gratin dishes. They can be
served hot as appetisers or side dishes, or let cool and
presented as healthy after-school treats for hungry
children or delicious snacks for the whole family.

Sformato di cavolfiore con olive
Cauliflower mould with black olives

Serves 4; Preparation: 25 minutes; Cooking: 55 minutes; Level of difficulty: Simple

Divide the cauliflower into large florets and trim the stems to about 12 mm (½ in). § Cook in a pot of salted, boiling water for 5-7 minutes. Don't let the florets turn mushy. Drain and set aside. § Prepare a fairly thick béchamel sauce. § Chop the cauliflower, place in a food mill, and purée. § Combine the purée with the béchamel, parmesan, olives, eggs, salt, pepper and nutmeg. § Grease the mould with a little butter and sprinkle with bread crumbs. Pour the mixture into the mould and place the mould in a larger container filled with water. § Cook in a preheated oven at 180°C /350°F for about 45 minutes. § Invert onto a platter while still hot. Serve hot or cold.

Sformato di spinaci
Spinach mould

Like all the moulds given here, Sformato di spinaci *can be served as a first or main course, or as a side dish with meat or fish. If you want to add a touch of colour to this spinach mould, garnish with 1 quantity of basic tomato sauce, well-reduced (see recipe p. 20).*

Serves 4; Preparation: 30 minutes; Cooking: 1 hour; Level of difficulty: Medium

Cook the spinach in a pot of salted, boiling water until tender (3-4 minutes if frozen, 8-10 minutes if fresh). Drain, cool under cold running water, and squeeze out excess moisture. Place in a food mill and purée. § Put the spinach in a saucepan with the cream and stir over medium heat until all the moisture has been absorbed. Remove from heat. § Prepare the béchamel sauce. Set aside to cool for 5 minutes. § Combine the béchamel with the spinach purée and add the parmesan, nutmeg and egg yolks. Season with salt and pepper. § Beat the egg whites until stiff and carefully fold them into the spinach mixture. § Grease the mould with a little butter and dust with flour. Pour the mixture into the mould. § Place the mould in a larger container filled with water and cook in a preheated oven at 180°C /350°F for about 45 minutes. § Invert onto a platter while still hot. Serve hot or cold.

■ INGREDIENTS

- 1 kg (2 lb) cauliflower head
- 1 quantity béchamel sauce (see recipe p. 26)
- salt and freshly ground black pepper
- ¼ teaspoon nutmeg
- 60 g (2 oz) freshly grated parmesan cheese
- 20 pitted and chopped black olives
- 3 eggs, beaten to a foam
- butter to grease the mould and bread crumbs
- ring mould 25-30 cm (10-12 in) in diameter

Wine: a dry white (Melissa)

■ INGREDIENTS

- 750 g (1½ lb) fresh or 500 g (1 lb) frozen spinach
- salt and freshly ground black pepper
- 60 ml (2fl oz) fresh cream
- 1 quantity béchamel sauce (see recipe p. 26)
- 30 g (1 oz) freshly grated parmesan cheese
- ¼ teaspoon nutmeg
- 2 eggs, separated
- butter and flour to grease and dust the mould
- ring mould 25-30 cm (10-12 in) in diameter

Wine: a dry white (Pinot grigio)

Right: *Sformato di spinaci con salsa di pomodoro*

SFORMATO DI ZUCCHINE CON CAROTE
Courgette and carrot mould

Serves 4-6; Preparation: 40 minutes; Cooking: 1½ hours; Level of difficulty: Medium

Put 100 g (3½ oz) of the courgettes in a sauté pan with 1 tablespoon of oil. Cook over medium heat for 5 minutes. Set aside. § Sauté the carrots and onions in the rest of the oil for 5 minutes. § Add the remaining courgettes, partially cover, and cook for 10-15 minutes, or until the vegetables are soft but not mushy. § Prepare the béchamel sauce. Let cool for 5-10 minutes. § Combine the béchamel with the parmesan, eggs, vegetables and mint. Season with salt and pepper. Mix well. § Grease the mould with the butter and sprinkle with bread crumbs. § Line the mould with the courgette wheels by sticking them one by one to the butter and bread crumbs until the entire mould is covered. § Pour the courgette mixture into the mould, taking care not to demolish the courgette mosaic. § Place the mould in a larger pan of water and cook in a preheated oven at 200°C/400°F for 50 minutes. § Let stand for 10 minutes, then invert on a serving dish. § Serve as a first course or side dish.

■ INGREDIENTS

- 650 g (1¼ lb) courgettes (zucchini), cut in wheels
- 4 tablespoons extra-virgin olive oil
- 2 medium onions, 4 medium carrots, finely chopped together
- 1 quantity béchamel sauce (see recipe p. 26)
- 60 g (2 oz) freshly grated parmesan cheese
- 2 eggs, beaten to a foam
- 2 tablespoons finely chopped fresh mint
- salt and freshly ground black pepper
- butter to grease the mould and bread crumbs
- ring mould 25-30 cm (10-12 in) in diameter

Wine: a dry white (Locorotondo)

GRATIN SOFFICE DI CIPOLLE
Fluffy onion gratin

Serves 4-6; Preparation: 30 minutes; Cooking: 1½ hours; Level of difficulty: Simple

Boil the potatoes in their skins in a pot of salted water for about 25 minutes. Drain and cover to keep warm. § Place the onions, oil, half the butter, wine, water, boullion cube, salt and pepper in a saucepan, cover and simmer for 35 minutes, or until the onions are soft. § Peel the potatoes, chop coarsely, and purée in a food mill. § Heat the milk in a saucepan and add the potatoes and the remaining butter (except 1 tablespoon) to make a smooth purée. § Remove from heat and let cool for 10 minutes. § Combine the purée with the eggs, salt and pepper. Stir in the parmesan (except 2 tablespoons), mixing well. § Butter an ovenproof dish and spread half the potato mixture on the bottom in an even layer. § Drain the cooked onions of any liquid and spread over the potatoes. Sprinkle with the gruyère and cover with the remaining potatoes. § Sprinkle with bread crumbs and parmesan. § Bake in a preheated oven at 180°C/350°F for 25 minutes. § Serve hot as a light lunch or side dish.

■ INGREDIENTS

- 1.5 kg (3 lb) potatoes
- 6 large onions, thickly sliced
- 1 tablespoon extra-virgin olive oil
- 100 g (3½ oz) butter
- 250 ml (8fl oz) dry white wine
- 125 ml (4fl oz) water
- 1 vegetable bouillon cube
- salt and freshly ground black pepper
- 300 ml (10 oz) milk
- 3 eggs, beaten to a foam
- 100 g (3½ oz) freshly grated parmesan cheese
- 100 g (3½ oz) freshly grated gruyère cheese
- 2 tablespoons bread crumbs

Wine: a dry red (Refosco)

Right: *Gratin soffice di cipolla*

- 1 medium cabbage
- 2 onions, 2 cloves garlic, finely chopped
- 2½ tablespoons extra-virgin olive oil
- 250 g (8 oz) parboiled rice
- 500 g (1 lb) peeled and chopped tomatoes
- 1 quantity béchamel sauce (see recipe p. 26)
- 200 g (7 oz) freshly grated gruyère cheese
- 1 tablespoon butter

Wine: a young red (Vino Novello)

GRATIN DELICATO DI VERZA E RISO
Cabbage, rice and tomato gratin

Serves 4-6; Preparation: 25 minutes; Cooking: 55 minutes; Level of difficulty: Simple

Discard the outer leaves of the cabbage and cut off the stalk. Divide in half and cut into strips. Blanch in salted, boiling water, drain well, and spread on a tea towel to dry. § Sauté the onion and garlic with the oil in a sauté pan. § Stir in the rice and season with salt and pepper. § Add the tomatoes and cook for 15 minutes, or until the rice is cooked *al dente*. § Prepare the béchamel and add half the gruyère. § Grease an ovenproof dish and alternate layers of cabbage with layers of rice and tomatoes. § Cover with the béchamel and sprinkle with the remaining cheese. Bake in a preheated oven at 180°C/350° F for 30 minutes.

Melanzane farcite piccanti
Aubergines filled with provolone cheese

Serves 4; Preparation: about 1½ hours; Cooking: 40 minutes; Level of difficulty: Simple

Cut the aubergines in half lengthwise and make crosswise slits in the pulp without piercing the skin. Sprinkle with salt and place the halves face upward in a large flat dish. Cover with another dish facing upward and put a weight on top. Leave for at least 1 hour so that the bitter liquid can run off. § Drain and rinse under running water, squeeze gently and place face down on paper towels to dry. § Mix the garlic, pancetta and the two provolone cheeses in a bowl. § Place the aubergines in an ovenproof braiser with the oil. Press the aubergines open and distribute the filling in the slits made earlier with the knife. § Cover with tomato pulp and sprinkle with parmesan. Season with pepper (don't add salt, as the aubergines have already absorbed enough). § Drizzle a little oil over the top. § Pour the broth into the bottom of the braiser and cook over medium-low heat for 10-15 minutes. § Transfer to a preheated oven and bake at 180°C/350°F for 25-30 minutes. Baste with the broth from time to time. § Serve hot as a main course.

■ INGREDIENTS

- 6 long aubergines (eggplants)
- 60 g (2 oz) salt
- 8 cloves garlic, finely chopped
- 60 g (2 oz) pancetta, diced
- 150 g (5 oz) sharp provolone cheese and 150 g (5 oz) mild provolone cheese, diced
- 600 g (20 oz) chopped tinned tomatoes
- freshly ground black pepper
- 6 tablespoons freshly grated parmesan cheese
- 4 tablespoons extra-virgin olive oil
- 250 ml (8fl oz) meat or vegetable broth (see recipe p. 24)

Wine: a dry white (Tocai)

Parmigiana di melanzane
Aubergine in tomato sauce with parmesan and mozzarella cheese

A classic Italian recipe, originally from Sicily. It is a hearty dish and can be served as a complete main course. Try replacing the aubergine with 1.5 kg (3 lb) of courgettes for a lighter dish.

Serves 6-8; Preparation: about 1¼ hours; Cooking: 50 minutes; Level of difficulty: Simple

Peel the aubergines and cut in 6 mm (¼-in) slices, sprinkle with salt and place in a flat dish. Cover with another dish facing upward with a weight on top. Leave for at least 1 hour until the bitter liquid has run off. § Drain and rinse in cold water. Pat dry with a tea towel. § Prepare the tomato sauce. § Dredge the aubergines in the flour. § Heat the oil in a large sauté pan, dip the aubergine slices in the egg mixture and fry until golden brown. § Place on paper towels. § Place a layer of tomato sauce in the bottom of an ovenproof dish and cover with a layer of aubergine and a layer of mozzarella and parmesan. Repeat until you have several layers of each. Keep a little tomato sauce and parmesan to spread on top. § Dot with butter and bake in a preheated oven at 180°C/350°F for 35 minutes. § Serve hot from the baking dish as a main course.

■ INGREDIENTS

- 60 g (2 oz) salt
- 4 large round aubergines (eggplants)
- 2 quantities basic tomato sauce (see recipe p. 20)
- plain flour to dredge
- 4 eggs, beaten to a foam with a pinch of salt
- 3 cups oil, for frying
- 300 g (12 oz) mozzarella cheese
- 200 g (6½ oz) freshly grated parmesan cheese
- 2 tablespoons butter

Wine: a dry red (Santa Cristina)

Right:
Parmigiana di melanzane

GRATIN DI BELGA E PROSCIUTTO
Belgian endives baked in béchamel sauce

■ INGREDIENTS

- 8 medium heads Belgian endives
- 3 tablespoons extra-virgin olive oil
- 125 ml (4fl oz) water
- salt
- 1 quantity béchamel sauce (see recipe p. 26)
- salt and freshly ground black pepper
- 1 tablespoon butter to grease the pan
- 8 thick slices ham
- 90 g (3 oz) freshly grated gruyère cheese

Wine a dry red (Chianti Castelgreve)

Serves 4-8; Preparation: 40 minutes; Cooking: 1 hour; Level of difficulty: Simple

Using a sharp knife, hollow out the base of the endives to remove the bitter part and ensure uniform cooking. § Place the heads in a large pan with the oil, water and salt to taste. Cover and braise over medium heat for about 40 minutes. Drain well. § Prepare the béchamel sauce. § Wrap each endive in a slice of ham and arrange the heads in a greased ovenproof dish (take care to place the part where the ham overlaps underneath). § Pour the béchamel over the rolls and sprinkle gruyère over the top. § Bake in a preheated oven at 180°C/350°F for 25 minutes, or until the topping turns golden brown. § Serve hot directly from the baking dish as an appetiser or side dish.

POMODORI IN VERDE
Tomatoes baked with parmesan, parsley and garlic

■ INGREDIENTS

- 10 medium tomatoes
- 5 cloves garlic, finely chopped
- 10 tablespoons finely chopped parsley
- 6 tablespoons bread crumbs
- 6 tablespoons freshly grated parmesan cheese
- 6 tablespoons extra-virgin olive oil.
- salt and freshly ground black pepper

Wine: a young dry red (Bardolino)

Left: *Pomodori in verde*

Serves 4-6; Preparation: 35 minutes; Cooking: 35 minutes; Level of difficulty: Simple

Cut the tomatoes in half, remove the seeds with your fingers, sprinkle with a little salt, and place upside down in a colander for 20 minutes. § Mix the garlic and parsley together in a bowl, add the bread crumbs and parmesan, and work the oil in little by little using a fork. Season with salt and pepper. § Using a teaspoon, push the filling mixture into the tomato halves. Press it down with your fingers so that it sticks to the inside of the tomatoes (it will swell slightly in the oven and could overflow). § Place the filled tomatoes in a greased ovenproof dish and bake in a preheated oven at 180°C/350°F for 35 minutes. § Serve hot or warm as an appetiser or a side dish with roast beef or lamb chops. Perfect also with baked fish.

Crêpes farcite con bietolina e caprino
Crêpes stuffed with Swiss chard and caprino cheese

Serves 4-6; Preparation: 60 minutes; Cooking: 30 minutes; Level of difficulty: Medium

Prepare the crêpes and set aside. § Cook the chard in a pot of salted water for 5 minutes. Drain, squeeze and chop finely. § Sauté the garlic with the butter in a sauté pan until golden in colour and remove. § In the same pan, sauté the chard with a pinch of salt for 5 minutes. § Prepare the béchamel. § Spread the caprino on the crêpes on the less browned side and grate a little nutmeg over the cheese. § Place 2 tablespoons of chard on half of each crêpe. § Fold each crêpe in half and then in half again to form a triangle. § Grease an ovenproof dish and arrange the crêpes overlapping inside. § Pour the béchamel sauce over the top and sprinkle with the gruyère. § Bake in a preheated oven at 180°C/350°F for 20-25 minutes. § Serve hot directly from the baking dish as a first course.

■ INGREDIENTS

- 12 crêpes (see recipe p. 26)
- 750 g (1½ lb) tender young Swiss chard
- salt and freshly ground black pepper
- 2 cloves garlic, cut in half
- 2 tablespoons butter
- 1 quantity béchamel sauce (see recipe p. 26)
- 250 g (8 oz) fresh caprino (goat's cheese)
- whole nutmeg to grate
- 60 g (2 oz) freshly grated gruyère cheese

Wine: a slightly sweet sparkling red (Brachetto d'Acqui)

Fagottini di melanzane alla carne
Aubergine stuffed with chicken, mortadella and ham

Serves 4; Preparation: 1½ hours; Cooking: 45 minutes; Level of difficulty: Simple

Cut the aubergines in 6 mm (¼-in) slices, sprinkle with salt and place in a flat dish. Cover with another dish facing upward with a weight on top. Leave for at least 1 hour until the bitter liquid has run off. § Drain and rinse under cold running water. Pat dry with a cotton tea towel. § In a bowl, blend the chicken, mortadella, prosciutto, parmesan, eggs, garlic, pepper and parsley. § Heat the oil in a sauté pan and fry the aubergine, turning the slices until they are golden brown. Drain on paper towels. § Arrange the slices on a clean work bench in pairs, crosswise one over the other. Place a little filling in the middle of each pair and fold the inner slice first, followed by the outer slice to form a little "package". Fasten with a wooden toothpick. § Sauté the onion in the olive oil in an ovenproof braiser for 5 minutes. Add the tomatoes, season with salt and pepper and cook for 5 more minutes. § Put the rolls in the braiser with the sauce and bake in a preheated oven at 180°C/350°F for 30 minutes. Baste with the sauce from time to time. § Serve hot as a main course with slices of toast rubbed with garlic, or boiled potatoes with a little of the tomato sauce.

■ INGREDIENTS

- 4 medium aubergines (eggplants)
- 60 g (2 oz) salt
- 150 g (5 oz) chicken breast, 100 g (3½ oz) mortadella, 150 g (5 oz) prosciutto, finely chopped
- 100 g (3½ oz) freshly grated parmesan cheese
- 1 egg + 1 yolk, beaten
- 2 tablespoons parsley, 3 cloves garlic, finely chopped
- freshly ground black pepper
- 500 ml (16fl oz) oil, for frying
- 1 onion, finely chopped
- 4 tablespoons extra-virgin olive oil
- 400 g (14 oz) tin tomatoes

Wine: a dry red (Chianti)

Right: Crêpes farcite con bietolina e caprino

- 6 medium courgettes (zucchini)
- 1 egg + 1 yolk, beaten
- 4 tablespoons freshly grated parmesan cheese
- 12 almond macaroons
- 2 tablespoons finely chopped parsley
- 2½ tablespoons extra-virgin olive oil
- 1 tablespoon butter
- 2 tablespoons bread crumbs

Wine: a dry white (Riesling)

ZUCCHINE FARCITE AGLI AMARETTI

Courgettes stuffed with almond macaroons

Serves 4; Preparation: 15 minutes; Cooking: 30 minutes; Level of difficulty: Simple

Cook the courgettes in a pot of salted, boiling water for 5 minutes. Drain and cool. § Cut in half lengthwise and, using a sharp knife, remove the pulp, leaving a 6 mm (¼-in) skin. § Crush the almond macaroons and place in a bowl with the eggs, chopped courgette pulp, parmesan, parsley and salt. Blend well with a fork. § Fill the courgettes and arrange them in a buttered baking dish. § Sprinkle with bread crumbs, drizzle with oil and bake in a preheated oven at 180°C/350° F for 25 minutes. § Serve hot as a first course.

Plum-cake di zucchine e fagiolini
Courgette and green bean pie

A savoury, Italian version of the celebrated British fruitcake.

Serves 6; Preparation: 30 minutes; Cooking: 1 hour; Level of difficulty: Medium

Cook the courgettes and beans in a pot of salted, boiling water for 10 minutes. Drain and cut the courgettes into wheels and the beans into pieces. Dry on a cotton tea towel. § Melt the butter and place in a bowl with two whole eggs, two yolks and the sugar. Beat vigorously for 2 minutes with a whisk or fork. Stir in the flour, courgettes, beans, pine nuts and baking powder. § Beat the remaining egg whites to stiff peaks and carefully fold into the mixture. § Grease a rectangular 20 cm (8 in) cake tin with butter and pour in the mixture. § Bake in a preheated oven at 180°C/350°F for about 50 minutes. § Remove from the tin when cool and cut into 12 mm (½-in) thick slices. § Serve slices as an appetiser or snack.

■ INGREDIENTS

• 300 g (10 oz) courgettes (zucchini)
• 250 g (8 oz) green beans
• 1 teaspoon salt
• 150 g (5 oz) butter
• 4 eggs
• 150 g (5 oz) sugar
• 300 g (10 oz) plain flour
• 125 g (4 oz) pine nuts
• 2 teaspoons baking powder
• butter to grease the cake tin

Wine: a dry red
(Sangiovese di Romagna)

Finocchi alla parmigiana
Baked fennel with parmesan cheese

Serves 4; Preparation: 15 minutes; Cooking: 25 minutes; Level of difficulty: Simple

Remove the outer leaves from each head of fennel, pare the tips and bottom, and cut in half. § Cook in salted, boiling water for 8-10 minutes, or until the fennel is cooked but still crunchy. § Drain, pat dry with paper towels, and cut into thick slices or wedges. § Place half the butter in a sauté pan and melt over low heat. Dredge the fennel slices lightly in the potato starch and cook over medium heat until crisp and golden brown. § Arrange in layers in a buttered baking dish. Sprinkle with salt, pepper and parmesan and dot with the remaining butter. § Bake in a preheated oven at 200°C/400°F for 15 minutes. § Serve hot as a first course or a side dish with oven-roasted fish or meat.

■ INGREDIENTS

• 5 large heads fennel
• salt and freshly ground black pepper
• 75 g (2½ oz) butter
• 5 tablespoons potato starch or plain flour
• 100 g (3½ oz) freshly grated parmesan cheese

Wine: a dry white
(Soave)

VARIATION
– For a richer dish: boil, slice and dry the fennel as above, then add 1 finely chopped small onion and brown with the sliced fennel (add more butter if necessary). When brown, add 150 g (5 oz) diced ham, 4 tablespoons fresh cream, and season with salt and pepper. Cover and let the sauce reduce over low heat for about 15 minutes. Sprinkle with 150 g (5 oz) freshly grated parmesan and bake as above.

Right:
Porri gratinati al prosciutto

INGREDIENTS

- 1 kg (2 lb) fresh leeks
- salt and freshly ground black pepper
- 1 quantity béchamel sauce (see recipe p. 26)
- 1 tablespoon butter
- 1 egg yolk
- 125 g (4 oz) ham, chopped
- 60 g (2 oz) freshly grated gruyère cheese

Wine: a dry white (Tocai di Lison)

Porri gratinati al prosciutto
Baked leeks with béchamel sauce and chopped ham

Serves 4-6; Preparation: 15 minutes; Cooking: 35 minutes; Level of difficulty: Simple

Discard any withered leaves from the leeks and chop off the green tops. Cook in salted, boiling water for 10 minutes, or until the leeks are cooked *al dente*. § Prepare the béchamel (with nutmeg) and leave to cool. § Drain the leeks and sauté for 5 minutes in a sauté pan with the butter, salt and pepper. Transfer to an ovenproof dish. § Combine the egg yolk and three-quarters of the ham with the béchamel, mix well, and pour over the leeks. Sprinkle with the gruyère and remaining ham. § Bake in a preheated oven at 180°C/350°F for 20 minutes. § Serve hot as a first course or side dish with meat or fish.

Patate gratinate con prosciutto e noci
Baked potatoes with béchamel, ham and walnuts

Serves 4-6; Preparation: 20 minutes; Cooking: 50 minutes; Level of difficulty: Simple
Cook the potatoes in their skins in salted, boiling water for about 25 minutes. Drain and set aside to cool. § Prepare a rather thick béchamel sauce and stir in the parmesan. § Peel the potatoes and cut in 12 mm (½-in) thick slices. Grease an ovenproof dish with butter and cover the bottom with a layer of potatoes. Fill in the gaps so that the bottom is sealed. § Spread with a layer of béchamel and sprinkle with the ham and chopped walnuts. Cover with another layer of potatoes, the mozzarella and a little béchamel sauce. Make a top layer of potatoes and cover with the remaining béchamel. Sprinkle with the bread crumbs and dot with the remaining butter. § Bake in a preheated oven at 180°C/350°F for about 25 minutes. § Garnish with remaining walnut halves and serve hot at lunch with a salad.

Torta di zucca e patate
Potato and pumpkin pie

Serves 4; Preparation: 20 minutes; Cooking: 1¼ hours; Level of difficulty: Simple
Peel the pumpkin and cut it in slices. Cover with foil and bake in a preheated oven at 150°C/300°F for about 25 minutes, or until soft. § Boil the potatoes in their skins for about 25 minutes, drain and peel. § Purée the potatoes and pumpkin together in a food mill. § Stir in half the butter, then add the egg yolks and parmesan. Mix rapidly, and season with salt and pepper. § Beat the egg whites to stiff peaks and fold them into the mixture. § Grease an ovenproof dish with butter and sprinkle with bread crumbs. § Spread half the mixture evenly in the bottom of the dish and cover with the mozzarella. Cover with the rest of the mixture. § Use a spoon to level, sprinkle with the parmesan, dot with the remaining butter and bake in a preheated oven at 180°C/350°F for 50 minutes. § Serve hot with a green salad as a main course or light lunch, or as side dish with roast lamb or grilled pork.

■ INGREDIENTS

- 1 kg (2 lb) potatoes
- salt and freshly ground black pepper
- 1 quantity béchamel sauce (see recipe p. 26)
- 60 g (2 oz) freshly grated parmesan cheese
- 2 tablespoons butter
- 200 g (7 oz) finely chopped ham
- 200 g (7 oz) shelled walnuts, almost all coarsely chopped
- 200 g (7 oz) mozzarella cheese, thinly sliced
- 1 tablespoon bread crumbs

Wine: a dry red (Dolcetto D'Alba)

■ INGREDIENTS

- 500 g (1 lb) pumpkin
- 500 g (1 lb) potatoes
- 75 g (2½ oz) butter
- 4 eggs, separated
- 100 g (3½ oz) freshly grated parmesan cheese
- salt and freshly ground black pepper
- 2 tablespoons bread crumbs
- 375 g (12 oz) mozzarella cheese, sliced

Wine: a dry red (Barbaresco)

Right: *Patate gratinate con prosciutto e noci*

CIPOLLE FARCITE DI RISO INTEGRALE
Onions stuffed with brown rice and oregano

Serves 4; Preparation: 25 minutes; Cooking: 1½ hours; Level of difficulty: Medium

Peel the onions, trim the bottoms and slice off the tops. Cook for 7-8 minutes in a pot of salted, boiling water. Set aside to cool on paper towels. § Cook the rice in a large pot of salted, boiling water and drain. § Hollow out the onions with a sharp knife leaving a 12 mm (½-in) thick shell. Set the pulp aside. § Beat the eggs in a bowl, and add the rice, half the oregano, the parmesan, pecorino, chopped olives, salt and pepper. Mix well. § Spoon the filling into the onions and sprinkle with the remaining oregano. § In a bowl, mix 4 tablespoons of onion pulp, the halved olives, 1 tablespoon of olive oil, salt and pepper, and pour into an ovenproof dish. § Arrange the stuffed onions in the dish and pour the remaining oil, wine and broth over the top. Dot each onion with butter and bake in a preheated oven at 180°C/350°F for 40 minutes. § Serve hot as a first course.

■ INGREDIENTS

- 8 large onions
- salt and freshly ground black pepper
- 200 g (7 oz) brown rice
- 3 eggs
- 2 tablespoons oregano
- 60 g (2 oz) freshly grated parmesan cheese
- 100 g (3½ oz) grated percorino romano cheese
- 200 g (7 oz) pitted black olives – 150 g (5 oz) coarsely chopped, 50 g (2 oz) cut in half
- 5 tablespoons extra-virgin olive oil
- 250 ml (8fl oz) white wine
- 250 ml (8fl oz) vegetable broth (see recipe p. 24)
- 2 tablespoons butter

Wine: a dry red (Freisa d'Asti)

CIUFFETTI DI PATATE E SPINACI
Spinach and potato appetisers

Serves 8; Preparation: 30 minutes; Cooking: 1 hour; Level of difficulty: Medium

Boil the potatoes in their skins for about 25 minutes. § Drain, peel and purée in a food mill. § Put the purée in a saucepan and add 80 g (3 oz) of butter, salt, pepper, nutmeg and milk. Place over a low heat and, stirring constantly, dry out excess moisture. Set aside to cool. § Cook the spinach in a pot of salted, boiling water until tender (3-4 minutes if frozen, 8-10 minutes if fresh). Drain well and squeeze out excess moisture. Purée in the food mill. § Beat the egg and one yolk together and mix well with the potato purée. § Divide the potato purée in two and mix the spinach and a dash of salt into one half. If the mixture is too moist, stir over low heat to dry. § Grease a baking sheet, spoon the potato mixture into the pastry bag, and squeeze out into walnut-sized rosettes. Repeat with the spinach mixture. § Beat the remaining egg yolk and brush the rosettes with it. § Bake in a preheated oven at 200°C/400°F for 20 minutes. § Scoop the rosettes off the sheet with a spatula and serve hot as appetisers.

■ INGREDIENTS

- 1 kg (2 lb) potatoes
- 100 g (3½ oz) butter
- salt and freshly ground black pepper
- dash of nutmeg
- 250 ml (8fl oz) milk
- 500 g (1 lb) fresh or 375 g (12 oz) frozen spinach
- 1 egg + 2 yolks
- pastry bag and tip or syringe

Wine: a dry sparkling red (Lambrusco)

Right:
Cipolle farcite di riso integrale

■ INGREDIENTS

- 1 quantity flaky pastry
  (see recipe p. 22)
- 2 red peppers
- 4 courgettes (zucchini)
- 4 large carrots
- salt and freshly ground
  black pepper
- 3 tablespoons extra-virgin
  olive oil
- 2 tablespoons butter
- 125 ml (4fl oz) white
  wine
- 500 g (1 lb) dried beans
  or chick peas
- a round or oval pie plate,
  25 cm (10 in) diameter

*Wine: a dry white
(Est! Est!! Est!!! di Montefiascone)*

■ INGREDIENTS

- 1 quantity flaky pastry
  (see recipe p. 22)
- 6 large onions, thinly sliced
- 30 g (1 oz) butter
- 500 ml (16fl oz) white wine
- 250 ml (8fl oz) vegetable
  broth (see recipe p. 24),
  or water
- 1 beef bouillon cube
- 500 g (1 lb) dried beans
  or chick peas
- ¾ cup fresh creamy
  cheese, such as robiola or
  mascarpone
- 1 teaspoon fresh or dried
  mint or lemon balm
- a round or oval pie plate,
  25 cm (10 in) diameter

Wine: a dry white (Tocai)

Left: *Crostata di verdure miste*

CROSTATA DI VERDURE MISTE
Vegetable pie

Serves 6; Preparation: 20 minutes (+ 1½ hours for the pastry); Cooking: 1 hour; Level of difficulty: Simple

Prepare the pastry dough. § Cut the peppers in thin strips, the courgettes in wheels and the carrots in ribbons. § Sauté the peppers, a pinch of salt and the oil in a sauté pan over high heat for 10 minutes, stirring frequently. Take the peppers out and set aside. § Use the same oil to sauté the courgettes with a pinch of salt. Remove from the sauté pan and set aside. § Use a paper towel to eliminate the oil in the pan. Put the butter, carrots, wine and a pinch of salt in it and cook until the liquid has evaporated and the carrots are soft. Set the carrots aside. § On a clean, lightly floured work bench, roll out the pastry dough and line a greased ovenproof pie plate with borders at least 2.5 cm (1 in) high. Prick the dough with a fork. § Cover the pie crust with a sheet of foil, weigh it down with dried beans, and bake in a preheated oven at 190°C/375°F for 35 minutes. § Remove the foil and beans and bake for 10 minutes more. § Arrange the vegetables over the pastry. § Slice and serve as an appetiser, or as a light lunch with a platter of fresh creamy cheeses (ricotta, mozzarella, robiola, caprino or mascarpone).

CROSTATA DI CIPOLLA
Onion pie

Serves 6; Preparation: 20 minutes (+ 1½ hours for the pastry); Cooking: 1 hour; Level of difficulty: Simple

Prepare the pastry dough. § Cook the onions in a sauté pan with the butter and season with salt and pepper. When the onions are soft, add the wine, and then the vegetable broth and bouillon cube. § Simmer over medium-low heat for at least 30 minutes, or until the onions are creamy. If the liquid evaporates during cooking, add water or broth. § On a clean, lightly floured work bench, roll out the pastry dough and line a greased ovenproof pie plate with borders at least 2.5 cm (1 in) high. Prick the dough with a fork. § Cover the pie crust with a sheet of foil, weigh it down with dried beans, and bake in a hot oven at 190°C/375°F for 35 minutes. § Remove the foil and beans and bake for 10 minutes more. § Set aside to cool, then spread with creamy cheese. § Spread the onion cream over the cheese and sprinkle with the mint or lemon balm. § Serve slices as an appetiser or snack.

CROSTATA DI BROCCOLI E PORRI
Broccoli and leek pie

*Both the broccoli and leek pie and the pea and artichoke pie
(see variation) freeze well. Prepare them ahead of time.
They make a delicious lunch for unexpected guests.*

Serves 6; Preparation: 1 hour (+ 1 hour for the pastry); Cooking: 1½ hours; Level of difficulty: Medium

Prepare the pastry dough and set it aside in the refrigerator. § Cut the roots and the green tops off the leeks and chop the white parts into fairly thin wheels. § Put the leeks in a sauté pan with the oil, cover and cook for 15 minutes, stirring frequently. Remove from heat and set aside. § Dry the oil in the pan with paper towels and sauté the pancetta until crispy and brown. Set aside. § Divide the broccoli into florets, leaving 12 mm (½-in) stems and cook in a pot of salted, boiling water for 7-10 minutes, or until they are cooked *al dente* (not mushy). § Roll out the pastry dough and line a greased pie plate. Press the dough into the bottom and sides so it sticks to the plate. Prick well with a fork. Cover with a sheet of foil, higher than the sides. § Fill with the dried beans (to keep the shell flat and prevent it from swelling during baking). § Bake in a preheated oven at 180°C/350°F for 15 minutes, remove the foil and dried beans and bake for 5 minutes more. § In the meantime, beat the eggs in a bowl and add the milk, cream, parmesan, salt and pepper. Beat with a whisk until frothy. § Put the leeks and broccoli in the baked pie shell, sprinkle with the pancetta and pour the eggs and cheese over the top. § Bake in a preheated oven at 180°C/350°F, turning the pie dish from time to time to make sure it cooks evenly. After 35 minutes check if the cream is cooked by sticking a toothpick into it; if it comes out damp, cook for 5-10 minutes more. § Serve hot as an appetiser or first course.

VARIATION
– An alternative pie can be made by replacing the leeks and broccoli with peas and artichokes. Prepare the peas (250 g/8 oz) and 4 artichokes as in the recipes *Piselli primavera al prezzemolo e prosciutto* (see p. 52) and *Spezzatino di carciofi* (see p. 42). The vegetables should be well drained of their cooking juices before placing them in the pie shell. Cover with the cream of eggs and cheese and bake and serve as above.

■ INGREDIENTS

- 1 quantity plain pastry (see recipe p. 22)
- 2 medium leeks
- 1½ tablespoons extra-virgin olive oil
- 150 g (5 oz) pancetta, diced
- 500 g (1 lb) broccoli
- butter to grease the pie plate
- salt and freshly ground black pepper
- 500 g (1 lb) dried beans or chick peas
- 3 eggs + 2 yolks
- 375 ml (12fl oz) milk
- 250 ml (8fl oz) cream
- 100 g (3½ oz) freshly grated parmesan cheese
- a round or oval pie plate, 25 cm (10 in) diameter

*Wine: a dry white
(Isonzo Sauvignon)*

Right:
Crostata di broccoli e porri

FRIED VEGETABLES

Even in tolerant Italy, serving crispy-fried golden vegetables is considered rather sinful. But by following one or two simple rules (see p. 15 for instructions on how to fry vegetables), the damage can be kept to a minimum. Fried vegetables need to be eaten hot, so prepare them ahead of time and serve them as soon as possible.

Zucca fritta alla menta e pinoli
Fried squash with mint and pine nuts

■ INGREDIENTS

- 1 kg (2 lb) peeled squash
- 100 g (3½ oz) plain flour
- 500 ml (16fl oz) oil, for frying
- 3 cloves garlic, sliced
- 30 fresh mint leaves
- 16 anchovy fillets
- salt and freshly ground black pepper
- 3 tablespoons extra-virgin olive oil
- 2 tablespoons apple vinegar
- 60 g (2 oz) pine nuts, sautéed in oil for 3 minutes

Wine: a young dry white (Malvasia)

Serves 4; Preparation: 20 minutes; Cooking: 30 minutes; Level of difficulty: Simple

Cut the squash into small 5 x 2.5 cm (2 x 1 in) pieces. Flour lightly and heat the oil to frying point (see How to Fry Vegetables p. 15). § Fry a few pieces at a time for 7-8 minutes each. When the pieces are cooked, set aside on paper towels. § Clean the oil, top up if necessary, and repeat until all the squash is cooked. § Place on a serving dish and sprinkle with the garlic, half the mint, the anchovy fillets, salt and pepper. Dress with the olive oil and vinegar, and mix carefully. Set aside to marinate for at least 3 hours. § Add the pine nuts and remaining mint just before serving.

Pomodori verdi fritti
Crispy-fried green tomatoes

■ INGREDIENTS

- 6 large green tomatoes
- 125 g (4 oz) plain flour
- 4 eggs, beaten to a foam
- 300 g (10 oz) bread crumbs
- 80 ml (3fl oz) beer
- 500 ml (16fl oz) oil, for frying
- salt

Wine: a dry red (Chianti Classico)

This dish comes from Tuscany, where it is served often throughout the summer months.

Serves 4-6; Preparation: 15 minutes; Cooking: 40-50 minutes; Level of difficulty: Simple

Cut the tomatoes into 12 mm (½-in) thick slices. Discard the first and last slices with skin on one side. § Place four bowls side by side and fill the first with the flour, the second with the eggs and beer, and the last two with bread crumbs. § Place two-thirds of the oil in a deep-sided sauté pan over medium heat and heat to frying point (see How to Fry Vegetables p. 15). § Dip the tomato slices into the flour; make sure they are well-coated and shake off any excess. Flour all the slices and set them on paper towels. Don't lay the floured slices on top of each other. § Immerse the slices in the egg, turn a couple of times, drain and pass to the first bowl of bread crumbs. Turn several times until they are well-coated. § Repeat with the second bowl of bread crumbs (which are drier). § Place 4 or 5 slices in the hot oil and fry for about 10 minutes, or until they are golden brown. Turn them over carefully at least twice using tongs or two forks. § Clean the oil of any residue and top up if necessary. Continue to fry until all the tomatoes are cooked. § Place the fried slices on paper towels and sprinkle with salt. § Serve hot on a heated serving dish as an appetiser or side dish with mixed grilled meats.

Right:
Pomodori verdi fritti

FAGOTTINI DI BIETOLA E SPINACI
Swiss chard and spinach fritters

- 1 quantity plain pastry (see recipe p. 22)
- 375 g (12 oz) fresh or 250 g (8 oz) frozen Swiss chard
- 375 g (12 oz) fresh or 250 g (8 oz) frozen spinach
- salt and freshly ground black pepper
- 2 eggs + 1 yolk
- 250 g (8 oz) ricotta cheese, crumbled
- 185 g (6 oz) diced mozzarella cheese
- 100 g (3½ oz) freshly grated parmesan cheese
- 500 ml (16fl oz) oil, for frying

Wine: a young, dry red (Rosso di Montalcino)

Serves 6; Preparation: 30 minutes (+ 1 hour for the pastry); Cooking: 50 minutes; Level of difficulty: Simple
Prepare the pastry dough. § Cook the chard and spinach in a pot of salted, boiling water until tender (3-4 minutes if frozen, 8-10 minutes if fresh). Drain, cool under cold running water, squeeze out excess moisture, and chop finely. § Beat the 2 eggs in a bowl and add the ricotta, mozzarella, parmesan, salt and pepper. Mix well. § Add the chard and spinach and mix well. § Roll the pastry dough out on a clean, floured work bench until very thin. Cut into squares of about 4 inches. § Place a little filling at the centre of each and fold in half. Beat the remaining egg yolk and brush the edges of each square before pressing firmly to seal. § Heat the oil in a large deep-sided sauté pan to frying point (see How to Fry Vegetables p. 15). § Place a few fritters gently in the oil and cook for about 10 minutes, or until golden brown. Turn using tongs or two spoons. Repeat until all the fritters are cooked. § Serve hot as an appetiser.

CAVOLFIORE FRITTO MARINATO
Fried cauliflower florets served with vinegar marinade

- 1 small cauliflower (about 500 g (1 lb), divided in florets
- salt and freshly ground black pepper
- 3 eggs, beaten to a foam
- 60 ml (2fl oz) beer
- 500 ml (16fl oz) oil, for frying
- 100 g (3½ oz) plain flour
- 250 ml (8fl oz) white wine vinegar
- 2 shallots, chopped
- 8 leaves fresh or ½ teaspoon dry thyme

Wine: a dry red (Pinot Nero)

Left:
Cavolfiore fritto marinato

Serves 4; Preparation: 15 minutes; Cooking: 40 minutes; Level of difficulty: Simple
Cook the cauliflower florets in a pot of salted, boiling water for 4-5 minutes, or until they are cooked *al dente*. Drain well, and place on a cotton tea towel to dry. § Combine the beaten eggs with the beer. § Place the oil in a sauté pan over medium heat and heat to frying point (see How to Fry Vegetables p. 15). § Place the flour in a bowl, dip the florets in, turn a few times and shake off excess. § When the oil is hot, immerse about 8-10 florets in the egg mixture. Coat well and transfer to the pan. § Turn a couple of times with two forks or tongs. Fry for about 10 minutes, or until golden brown on all sides. § Remove from the sauté pan and set aside on paper towels. § Repeat until all the florets are fried. Sprinkle with salt. § To prepare the marinade, place the vinegar in a small saucepan with the shallots. Boil for 5-6 minutes, then add the thyme and remove from heat. Pour into a serving bowl. § Serve the marinade and cauliflower florets hot as an appetiser, or as a side dish with fried chicken or grilled or oven-roasted fish.

Crocchette di pomodoro
Tomato croquettes

Serves 4; Preparation: 15 minutes; Cooking: 30 minutes; Level of difficulty: Medium

Peel the tomatoes, squeeze out the seeds, chop coarsely, and set in a colander to drain. § Place the ricotta and egg yolk in a bowl and mix to a smooth paste. § Add the tomatoes, parsley, nutmeg, salt and pepper and mix well. § Prepare 3 separate bowls: one with the flour, one with the egg and one with the bread crumbs. § Heat the oil in a deep-sided sauté pan until hot, about 150°C/300°F (see How to Fry Vegetables p. 15). § Form the mixture into croquettes of about 5 x 2.5 cm (2 x 1 in). If the mixture is too runny, add 1-2 tablespoons bread crumbs or freshly grated parmesan cheese. § Roll the croquettes in the flour, dip in the egg, and roll in the bread crumbs. § Fry a few at a time for about 10 minutes, or until golden brown. Turn with tongs or a fork during cooking. § Use a slotted spoon to scoop them out and drain on paper towels. § Serve straight from the pan as appetisers.

■ INGREDIENTS

- 300 g (10 oz) fresh tomatoes
- 150 g (5 oz) ricotta cheese, crumbled
- 1 egg (beaten until foamy) + 1 yolk
- 1½ tablespoons finely chopped parsley
- nutmeg (to taste)
- salt and freshly ground black pepper
- 100 g (3½ oz) plain flour
- 100 g (3½ oz) bread crumbs
- 500 ml (16fl oz) oil, for frying

Wine: a dry fruity white (Vermentino)

Funghi porcini fritti

The classic Italian recipe calls for fresh, high-quality porcini mushrooms. If you can't get them, use fresh brown cremini or white mushrooms in their place. For a richer dish, coat the raw mushroom slices in batter (see recipe p. 24) and fry as below.

Serves 4; Preparation: 15 minutes; Cooking: 25 minutes; Level of difficulty: Simple

Trim the roots of the mushrooms and carefully peel the bottom of the stem if discoloured or slightly mouldy. § Detach the stems from the caps and wash quickly under cold running water, removing any dirt with your fingers. Set aside to dry on paper towels. § Cut the stems and caps in slices about 6 mm (¼-in) thick. § Dredge the slices in the flour, coating well, and shake to eliminate any excess. § Heat the oil to frying point (see How to Fry Vegetables p. 15) and fry a few pieces at a time until golden brown. Cook all the stems first, then the caps. § Drain on paper towels, sprinkle with salt and serve at once as an appetiser or side dish.

■ INGREDIENTS

- 650 g (1¼ lb) fresh porcini (or cremini or white) mushrooms
- 100 g (3½ oz) flour to dredge
- 500 ml (16fl oz) oil, for frying
- salt

Wine: a dry red (Carmignano)

Right: *Funghi porcini fritti*

Salvia Fritta
Fried fresh sage leaves

Don't use an iron sauté pan to fry the leaves because it could react chemically with the sage.

Serves 4; Preparation: 10 minutes; Cooking: instant frying at 180°C/350°F; Level of difficulty: Simple

Wash the leaves, pat dry with paper towels and dredge in the flour. § Dip in the egg and coat with bread crumbs. § Heat the oil to very hot (test with a leaf which should sizzle sharply) and add half the leaves. They will turn golden brown almost instantly. Turn them once, then scoop out with a slotted spoon. Drain on paper towels. § Sprinkle with salt and serve crunchy as an appetiser or snack. § For a sweeter version, add 1 teaspoon of sugar to the salt before sprinkling.

■ INGREDIENTS

- 40 large fresh sage leaves
- 2 tablespoons plain flour
- 1 large egg, beaten until foamy with a pinch of salt
- 100 g (3½ oz) bread crumbs
- 500 ml (16fl oz) oil, for frying
- salt

Wine: a medium (or sweet) sparkling white (Verduzzo)

CROCCHETTE DI SPINACI
Spinach croquettes

■ INGREDIENTS

- 1.5 kg (3 lb) boiling potatoes
- salt and freshly ground black pepper
- 500 g (1 lb) fresh or 375 g (12 oz) frozen spinach
- 1 egg + 1 yolk, beaten
- 60 g (2 oz) freshly grated parmesan cheese
- 150 g (5 oz) taleggio or fontina cheese, cut in 6 mm (¼-in) cubes
- 125 g (4 oz) bread crumbs
- 500 ml (16fl oz) oil, for frying

Wine: a dry white (Pinot grigio)

Serves 4-6; Preparation: 30 minutes; Cooking: 1 hour; Level of difficulty: Simple

Cook the potatoes in their skins in a pot of salted, boiling water for about 25 minutes. Drain, peel and purée in a food mill. § Cook the spinach in a pot of salted, boiling water until tender (3-4 minutes if frozen, 8-10 minutes if fresh). Drain, cool under cold running water, squeeze out excess moisture, and chop finely. § Combine with the potatoes and mix well. § Put the eggs in a bowl with the salt, pepper, potatoes, spinach and parmesan and blend with a fork until smooth. § Place a tablespoonful of the mixture in the palm of your hand. Press a cube of cheese in the middle and close the mixture round it in an oblong croquette. The cheese must be completely covered. § Roll in the bread crumbs. § Heat the oil in a deep-sided sauté pan until hot, about 150°C/300°F (see How to Fry Vegetables p. 15). § Cook the croquettes a few at a time, turning them in the oil until they turn golden brown all over. § Remove with a slotted spoon and drain on paper towels. Repeat until all the croquettes are cooked. § Serve hot as an appetiser or with a mixed salad as a main course.

> VARIATION
> – Replace the spinach with porcini mushrooms (see recipe *Funghi Porcini Trifolati* p. 50). In this case, either omit the cheese or use mozzarella.

FRITTELLE DI PATATE
Potato patties

■ INGREDIENTS

- 650 g (1¼ lb) potatoes
- 2 eggs, beaten until foamy
- 2 tablespoons plain flour or potato starch
- salt and freshly ground black pepper
- 500 ml (16fl oz) oil, for frying

Wine: a medium-dry rosé (Lagrein rosato)

Left: *Crocchette di spinaci*

Serves 4; Preparation: 15 minutes; Cooking: 15-20 minutes; Level of difficulty: Simple

Peel the potatoes and grate into julienne strips with a grater. Rinse them in plenty of cold water, drain well and spread on a cotton tea towel to dry. § Place the eggs, flour, salt and pepper in a bowl, add the potatoes and mix well. If the mixture is too runny, add a little more flour to thicken. § Heat the oil in a deep-sided sauté pan to frying point (see How to Fry Vegetables p. 15). Place 6-8 widely separated tablespoons of the mixture in the oil. Brown on one side then turn carefully and fry golden brown on the other. § Scoop the patties out with a slotted spoon and drain on paper towels. § Serve hot as an appetiser or as a side dish with fried meat or fish dishes.

Fritto misto estivo
Mixed fried summer vegetables

In winter, replace the summer vegetables with wedges of artichoke and fennel, carrots and potatoes cut in sticks and florets of broccoli. The procedure is the same except that the fennel and broccoli must be cooked first in salted, boiling water until al dente *and dried on paper towels before flouring.*

Serves 4-6; Preparation: 20 minutes; Cooking: 50 minutes; Level of difficulty: Simple

Cut the courgettes in half crosswise, and cut each half in quarters lengthwise. If you are using the long aubergines, slice in 6 mm (¼-in) wheels. If you are using the larger, pear-shaped aubergines, cut in 6 mm (¼-in) thick slices and cut each slice in halves or quarters (depending on how big they are). § Trim the stems of the courgette blooms and wash the flowers carefully. Place on paper towels to dry. § Put the flour in a large bowl next to another containing the eggs and beer. § Heat the oil in a deep-sided sauté pan to frying point (see How to Fry Vegetables p. 15). § Flour the vegetables, shake off any excess and dip in the egg. Shake off excess egg and fry. § Begin frying a few pieces at a time; if there are too many in the sauté pan at once they will stick to one another. § Turn the vegetables as they brown. When all the pieces are golden brown, scoop them up with a slotted spoon and drain on paper towels. Repeat until all the vegetables are cooked. § Sprinkle with salt and serve hot as a first course or as a side dish with fried or roast meat or fish dishes.

■ INGREDIENTS

- 4 courgettes (zucchini)
- 4 aubergines (eggplants)
- 12 large courgette flowers
- 250 g (8 oz) plain flour
- 4 beaten eggs
- 80 ml (3fl oz) beer
- 500 ml (16fl oz) oil, for frying
- salt

Wine: a medium-dry white (Frascati)

Anelli di cipolla croccanti
Crispy-fried onion rings

Serves 4; Preparation: 20 minutes (+ 1 hour for the batter); Cooking: 20 minutes; Level of difficulty: Simple

Prepare the batter. § Peel the onions and chop in 6 mm (¼-in) slices. Separate the rings and leave them to dry for a few minutes. § Heat the oil in a deep-sided sauté pan to frying point (see How to Fry Vegetables p. 15). § Beat the egg white to stiff peaks and fold into the batter. § Dip the rings in the batter one by one, let the excess batter drip off, and fry to golden brown, turning once or twice with tongs or a fork. Remember to keep the oil clean. § Drain on paper towels and sprinkle with salt. § Serve hot as an appetiser.

■ INGREDIENTS

- 4 medium onions
- 1 quantity batter (see recipe p. 24)
- 1 egg white
- 500 ml (16fl oz) oil, for frying

Wine: a dry, sparkling white (Prosecco di Conegliano)

Right:
Fritto misto estivo

GRILLED VEGETABLES

Cooking vegetables quickly in a grill pan (or over a barbecue) enhances their natural flavours. Experiment with the dishes here, then try grilling a selection of different vegetables together and serve with oil, finely chopped parsley and garlic as a light and healthy lunch, or as a second course after a hearty pasta dish. See p. 14 for instructions on successful grilling.

Melanzane alla griglia in olio piccante
Grilled aubergines in oil and chilli sauce

Aubergines are now available throughout the year, but for successful grilling be sure to use them in their natural season — summer — when their full, flagrant flavour is at its peak. They can be served al naturale (sprinkled with finely chopped parsley and garlic and bathed in olive oil) or with the delicious spicy sauce given here. Cover with oil and keep in the refrigerator; they will be good for several days.

Serves 4-6; Preparation: 15 minutes; Cooking: 20 minutes; Level of difficulty: Simple

Chop the ends off the aubergines and cut them in 12 mm (½-in) thick slices. § Heat the grill pan to very hot and place the slices on it. Press them down with a fork so the aubergine adheres to the grill pan. Turn the slices after about 30 seconds (they will have black stripes on the cooked side). Aubergine cooks quickly so don't let the slices dry out. § As soon as the pulp is soft, remove from the grill pan and arrange on the serving dish. § Put the chillies, salt and pepper in the oil and beat well with a fork. Cover and set aside. § When the aubergines are all cooked, pour the spicy oil over the top and garnish with the basil leaves. § For an even richer flavour, sprinkle the grilled aubergines with 1 tablespoon of fresh oregano. § Serve warm or cold as an appetiser or side dish with mixed grilled meats or fish.

■ INGREDIENTS

• 4 large round aubergines (eggplants)
• 2 finely chopped hot chili peppers, or 1 teaspoon crushed chillies
• salt and freshly ground black pepper
• 250 ml (8fl oz) extra-virgin olive oil
• 10 fresh basil leaves, torn

Wine: a dry red (Rossesse di Dolceacqua)

Involtini di zucchine grigliate
Stuffed courgette rolls

Serves 4; Preparation: 15 minutes; Cooking: 10 minutes; Level of difficulty: Simple

Trim the ends of the courgettes and cut them lengthwise in 3 mm (⅛-in) slices. § Heat the grill pan until hot and cook the slices over medium-high heat for about 3 minutes on each side. Transfer to a plate. § Put the caprino in a bowl and mash with a fork. Add the tuna and mix well. Season with salt and pepper, add the parsley and blend vigorously until the mixture is smooth. § Place 2-3 teaspoons of filling on each slice of courgette, add some basil and roll up, fastening with a wooden toothpick. § Place the rolls on a serving dish. Sprinkle with capers and basil leaves and drizzle with oil. § Serve cool as appetisers.

■ INGREDIENTS

• 4 large courgettes (zucchini)
• 350 g (12 oz) caprino cheese (or another fresh, creamy cheese)
• 150 g (5 oz) crumbled tinned tuna in olive oil
• salt and freshly ground black pepper
• 1 tablespoon finely chopped parsley
• 1½ tablespoons capers
• 15 basil leaves, torn
• 3 tablespoons extra-virgin olive oil

Wine: a dry white (Verduzzo)

VARIATION
— Garnish with sliced tomatoes and sprinkle with oregano to add a spicy fragrance to the dish.

Right: *Melanzane alla griglia in olio piccante*

■ INGREDIENTS

- 8 medium red tomatoes
- salt and freshly ground
  black pepper
- 2 tablespoons oregano
- 16 fresh basil leaves, torn
- 4 tablespoons extra-
  virgin olive oil

Wine: a dry red
(Refosco)

Pomodori rossi alla griglia
Grilled tomatoes

Serves 4; Preparation: 10 minutes; Cooking: 15 minutes; Level of difficulty: Simple

Cut the tomatoes in half and remove the seeds with your fingers. Stand the halves upside down for 2-3 minutes. § Heat the grill pan to high heat. § Sprinkle the tomatoes with salt, pepper and oregano. § Place the tomatoes on the grill pan skin-side-down and cook over high heat without turning for about 15 minutes, or until they are cooked. § Remove from the grill pan, place a basil leaf in the centre of each and drizzle with the oil. § Serve hot on toasted wholewheat or homemade bread as an appetiser or as a side dish with grilled meat or fish.

INGREDIENTS

- 2 courgettes (zucchini)
- 1 long aubergine (eggplant)
- 1 medium onion
- 1 small red, 1 small yellow, and 1 small green pepper
- 2½ tablespoons extra-virgin olive oil
- salt and freshly ground black pepper
- ½ teaspoon paprika
- juice of ½ lemon
- 1 teaspoon dried or 1 tablespoon chopped fresh herbs (oregano, mint, or thyme)

Wine: a sparkling dry white (Prosecco di Conegliano)

SPIEDINI MISTI VARIOPINTI
Skewered mixed vegetables

Serves 4; Preparation: 25 minutes (+ 2 hours marinating); Cooking: 20 minutes; Level of difficulty: Simple

Cut the courgettes in wheels. Chop the aubergine in thick slices, then divide them in 4. Divide the onion in 4 wedges, then cut each wedge in half. Cut the peppers in 4 cm (1½-in) squares. § Thread the vegetable pieces in colourful array on wooden skewers. Set them on a plate. Prepare at least two skewers per person. § Place the oil, salt, pepper, paprika, lemon juice and herbs in a small bowl and beat vigorously with a fork until the sauce is well mixed. § Pour over the skewers, cover with foil and marinate in the refrigerator for 2-3 hours. § Heat a grill pan over high heat until very hot, drain the skewers, and place half of them in the pan. Cook for about 10 minutes, turning them so that they brown on all sides. Repeat with the remaining skewers. § Serve hot as a side dish with grilled meats or fish, or garnish with squares of grilled polenta and serve as an appetiser.

INGREDIENTS

- 4 heads fresh Belgian endives
- 4 heads red radicchio
- salt and freshly ground black pepper
- 4 tablespoons extra-virgin olive oil

Wine: a light dry white (Soave Classico)

INSALATA BELGA E RADICCHIO ROSSO ALLA GRIGLIA
Grilled Belgian endives and radicchio

Belgian endives and radicchio are both part of the chicory family. Radicchio can be very bitter; try to buy the long tapering variety with mottled red leaves called Radicchio di Treviso (it looks a bit like romaine lettuce), which is less bitter and ideal for grilling.

Serves 4; Preparation: 10 minutes; Cooking: 15 minutes; Level of difficulty: Simple

Trim the bases of the Belgian endives and radicchio, remove any withered leaves, and cut the heads in half. § Heat a grill pan until very hot, then lower heat to medium and place the Belgian endives and radicchio in it. § Cover with a lid or sheet of foil during the first 5 minutes of cooking, then uncover and turn often until cooked. § Arrange the endives and radicchio in alternate red and white strips in a preheated serving dish. Sprinkle with salt and pepper and drizzle with the oil. § For a delicious and healthy light lunch, serve hot on a bed of boiled brown rice and garnish with wedges of cherry tomatoes and freshly grated pecorino romano cheese.

Left:

Spiedini misti variopinti

Porcini alla Griglia
Grilled wild mushrooms on toast with herb butter

The Italian recipe calls for fresh porcini, but you can use other wild mushrooms in their place.
Experiment with shiitake, chanterelle, hedgehog, cremini or portobello mushrooms (or a mixture).

Serves 4; Preparation: 10 minutes; Cooking: 10-15 minutes; Level of difficulty: Simple

Remove any dirt from the mushrooms, trim the tough parts off the stems, and rinse carefully under cold running water. Dry with paper towels. § Detach the stems and slice them in half lengthwise. Make small slits with a sharp knife in the caps and stems and insert the garlic and calamint. Make at least 4 slits per cap and 2 per stem. § Mix the oil, salt and pepper in a small bowl and drizzle it over the mushrooms. Set aside for a few minutes. § Place the butter, garlic, spring onions, parsley, salt and pepper in a small bowl and mix until smooth. Set aside. § Heat a grill pan to very hot and place the mushrooms in it, beginning with the stems (which may take a little longer to cook, depending on the type of mushroom). § Cook for 5-7 minutes, turning often so they don't stick. § Prepare slices of toast made with tasty wholewheat or homemade bread, spread with the herb butter and distribute the mushrooms on top. § Serve immediately as an appetiser or snack.

INGREDIENTS

- 750 g (1½ lb) whole fresh wild mushrooms (shiitake, chanterelle, hedgehog, cremini, portobello)
- 4 cloves garlic, sliced
- 4 tablespoons fresh or 2 tablespoons dried calamint (or thyme)
- salt and freshly ground black pepper
- 4 tablespoons extra-virgin olive oil
- 100 g (3½ oz) softened butter
- 1 clove garlic, finely chopped
- 1 tablespoon finely chopped spring onions
- 2 tablespoons finely chopped parsley
- 4-8 slices wholewheat or homemade bread

Wine: a dry red
(Chianti Classico)

Spiedini di Cipolline e Alloro
Skewered grilled onions with bay leaves

Serves 4; Preparation: 10 minutes; Cooking: 20 minutes; Level of difficulty: Simple

Blanch the onions in a pot of salted, boiling water for 5 minutes. § Drain, dry and thread onto 4 skewers (5 onions each, alternated with a half bay leaf). Skewer the onions horizontally so that they will lie flat in the grill pan during cooking. § Drizzle with oil and cook in a hot grill pan, turning often. Cook for about 15 minutes, or until the onions are golden brown. § Sprinkle with salt and pepper and serve as appetisers or with grilled sausages.

INGREDIENTS

- 20 small white onions, peeled
- 8 bay leaves, cut in half
- 1 tablespoon extra-virgin olive oil
- salt and freshly ground black pepper

Wine: a dry red (Pinot Nero)

Right: Spiedini di cipolline e alloro

Peperoni bruciati
Grilled peppers in garlic, parsley and oil

*Preparing this delicious dish takes a little time, but is definitely worth the effort.
The grilled peppers will keep in the refrigerator for about a week (cover well with oil),
so you can double or even triple the quantities given here.*

Serves 4; Preparation: 1 hour; Cooking: 30 minutes; Level of difficulty: Simple

Heat the grill pan to very hot. Place as many whole peppers in the pan as will fit and press with a lid. The skin of the peppers has to burn completely black. Turn them when one side is black. The peppers become soft as they cook; turn them often when they are soft to avoid burning the pulp. § Wrap each cooked pepper in 2-3 layers of paper towels (they are easier to peel if kept warm). § When all the peppers are cooked, remove the blackened skins using your fingers and paper towels. § Remove the core, stem, seeds and filaments. § Flatten the cleaned pieces and cut them into strips. § Place them on a serving dish and dress with the garlic, capers, basil, mint, salt and plenty of oil. § Mix carefully and set aside for at least an hour before serving. § Serve as an appetiser with slices of toasted wholewheat bread.

■ INGREDIENTS

- 5 large, fleshy, fresh peppers of different colours
- 5 cloves garlic, thinly sliced
- 150 g (5 oz) capers
- 20 fresh basil leaves, cut into strips
- 15 mint leaves, whole
- salt
- 10-12 tablespoons extra-virgin olive oil

*Wine: a dry red
(Recioto di Valpolicella)*

Cipolle grigliate con formaggio dolce fresco
Grilled onions filled with fresh creamy cheese

If you have an open fire or barbecue, bury the onions in the hot coals or ashes for about 35 minutes. They will have an even more delicious smoky flavour.

Serves 4; Preparation: 10 minutes; Cooking: 45 minutes; Level of difficulty: Simple

Trim the onions top and bottom, taking a larger slice from the top. § Wrap each onion in a piece of foil. § Heat the grill pan over high heat until very hot. Place the onions in it and lower heat to medium so that the onions cook slowly. Turn from time to time. § After about 45 minutes, pierce an onion through the centre with a wooden skewer. If it goes in easily, the onions are done; if the centre still feels hard or moist, continue cooking for another 5-10 minutes. § Remove from the grill and cut in half, season with oil, salt, pepper and place half a tablespoon of cheese in each half. § Serve hot with grilled pork chops or sausages.

■ INGREDIENTS

- 8 medium red or white onions
- 4 tablespoons extra-virgin olive oil
- salt and freshly ground black pepper
- 8 tablespoons fresh slightly sweet creamy cheese (marscapone)

*Wine: a dry red
(Leverano)*

Right: *Cipolle grigliate con formaggio dolce fresco*

- 4 aubergines (eggplants)
- 4 peppers
- 6 ripe tomatoes
- 3 cloves garlic, finely chopped
- 6 tablespoons extra-virgin olive oil
- salt and freshly ground black pepper
- 10 fresh basil leaves, torn

Wine: a dry white (Soave)

INSALATA GRIGLIATA
Grilled salad

Serves 6; Preparation: 10 minutes; Cooking: 45 minutes; Level of difficulty: Simple

Cut the aubergines in 12 mm (½-in) slices. § Heat the grill pan to very hot and cook the aubergines until tender. Set aside. § Cut the peppers in broad strips and cook in the grill pan, turning with a fork until they are cooked. Set aside. § Peel the tomatoes, cut them in half, and cook on the grill pan until they are pulpy. § Chop the aubergines and peppers in squares and place in a salad bowl with the tomatoes. § Sprinkle with salt, pepper, basil, garlic and oil. § Serve cool as a refreshing appetiser on hot summer nights.

Salads

Traditional Italian cuisine includes a plethora of delicious salads, from simple green and mixed dishes served after the main course to revive the palate, to more original regional salads, such as broad beans and pecorino cheese in Tuscany, and green salads with oranges in the citrus-growing South.

Pinzimonio
Platter of raw vegetables with oil, salt and pepper dip

Pinzimonio is a sort of do-it-yourself-salad. A platter of the season's raw vegetables, washed and cut into manageable pieces, is placed at the centre of the table and each guest is given a tiny bowl of oil, salt and pepper to dip the vegetables. Serve it as an appetiser with slices of toasted wholewheat or homemade bread or as a refreshing course in itself after a hearty meat dish. These are the traditional pinzimonio vegetables, but use your imagination and whatever you have available in the pantry or garden. Raw courgette sticks, sliced peppers, cherry tomatoes or cubes of cucumber (with toothpicks for dipping) are just a few that spring to mind.

Serves 4; Preparation: 20 minutes; Level of difficulty: Simple

Wash all the vegetables thoroughly under cold running water. § Artichokes: remove all but the pale inner leaves by pulling the outer ones down and snapping them off. Cut off the stem and the top third of the remaining leaves. Cut the artichokes in half lengthwise and scrape any fuzzy choke away with a knife. Cut each artichoke in wedges and soak in a bowl of cold water with the juice of 1 lemon for 10 minutes. § Carrots: scrub with a brush or peel and soak in a bowl of cold water with the remaining lemon juice for 10 minutes. § Celery: discard the stringy outer stalks and trim off the leafy tops. Keep the inner white stalks and the heart. § Fennel: slice off the base, trim away the leafy tops, and discard the blemished outer leaves. Divide into 4 or more wedges, depending on the size. § Onions: remove the roots and the outer leaves and trim the tops. § Radishes: cut the roots off and trim the tops. § For the dip: blend the oil with salt and pepper to taste with a whisk or blender. Pour into 4 small bowls.

■ INGREDIENTS

- 4 artichokes
- juice of 2 lemons
- 4 carrots (or 8 baby spring carrots)
- 4 celery hearts
- 2 large fennels
- 12 spring onions
- 12 radishes
- 300 ml (10fl oz) extra-virgin olive oil
- salt and freshly ground black pepper
- 1 tablespoon oregano (optional)

Wine: a light dry white (Verzemino)

Bagna Cauda
Hot Piedmont-style dip for raw vegetables

Serves 4-6; Preparation: 10 minutes; Cooking: 25 minutes; Level of difficulty: Simple

Place the garlic in a small pot with a pat of butter and a tablespoon of water. Simmer over very low heat, gradually adding all the butter; make sure the butter doesn't brown or the garlic fry. § Add the anchovy fillets and the oil, a little at a time. Mix well. § The dip is kept hot on the table in an earthenware pot over a warming apparatus (lacking all else, use a candle!). § Serve as a dip for raw vegetables. It is also good with cooked vegetables, grilled peppers and as a sauce for fresh pasta and potato gnocchi.

■ INGREDIENTS

- 6 cloves garlic, very finely chopped
- 60 g (2 oz) butter
- 300 ml (10fl oz) extra-virgin olive oil
- 20 anchovy fillets (best if packed under salt), finely chopped

Right:
Insalata aranciata

■ INGREDIENTS

- 3 fresh oranges
- 150 g (5 oz) arugula
- 150 g (5 oz) lamb's lettuce
- 2 medium red onions
- 100 g (3½ oz) pitted and chopped black olives
- 5 tablespoons extra-virgin olive oil
- 2 tablespoons red vinegar
- salt and black pepper

Wine: a dry sparkling red (Lambrusco di Sorbara)

INSALATA ARANCIATA
Arugula and oranges with olives and sweet red onions

Serves 4; Preparation: 20 minutes; Level of difficulty: Simple

Peel the oranges, discard any seeds and use a sharp knife to remove all the white part. Cut in thick slices and divide each slice in half. § Wash and dry the salad greens. § Cut the onions in thin slices. § Place the oranges, arugula, lamb's lettuce, onions and olives in a salad bowl. § Mix the oil, vinegar, salt and pepper together in bowl and pour over the salad. Toss well. § Set aside for 20 minutes before serving. § Serve as an appetiser or first course with toasted wholewheat or homemade bread.

Insalata di spinaci e grana
Raw spinach and parmesan salad

■ INGREDIENTS

- 400 g (13 oz) dwarf spinach, tender and very fresh
- 2 carrots, peeled
- 250 g (8 oz) tinned corn kernels, or 8 baby corn cobs
- 150 g (5 oz) parmesan cheese, in flakes
- ½ teaspoon salt
- juice of 1 lemon
- 4 tablespoons extra-virgin olive oil
- freshly ground black pepper

Wine: a dry white (Biondello del Metauro)

Serves 4; Preparation: 15 minutes; Level of difficulty: Simple

Trim the stems and discard any bruised spinach leaves, wash thoroughly, drain and dry on a cotton tea towel. § Grate the carrots in julienne strips. § Place the spinach in a large round dish or low, wide salad bowl and sprinkle with the carrots and corn. § Top with the flakes of parmesan. § In a small bowl, dissolve the salt in the lemon juice, add the oil and pepper and whisk to blend. § Dress the salad 5 minutes before serving. § This salad makes an eyecatching appetiser, but can also be served as a side dish with grilled fish or veal cutlets sautéed in white wine and lemon.

> VARIATION
> – Add a small honeydew melon in balls (made with a melon baller) or cubes, and 150 g (5 oz) of lean prosciutto in strips.

Asparagi in insalata
Asparagus salad

This tasty salad is also good with homemade mayonnaise (see recipe p. 28)

■ INGREDIENTS

- 1 kg (2 lb) asparagus
- 6 heads red radicchio
- 250 g (8 oz) thinly sliced white mushrooms
- ½ teaspoon salt
- peel of 2 lemons, finely chopped with 10 basil leaves
- 6 tablespoons extra-virgin olive oil
- 3 tablespoons lemon juice
- freshly ground black pepper

Wine: a dry white (Gambellara)

Right: *Insalata di spinaci e grana*

Serves 4; Preparation: 20 minutes; Cooking: 10 minutes; Level of difficulty: Simple

Trim the tough parts off the asparagus stalks and blanch for 7-10 minutes in a pot of salted, boiling water. Drain well and set aside to cool. § Wash and dry the radicchio and detach the leaves. § Arrange a bed of radicchio leaves on a serving dish and scatter with the mushrooms. Arrange the asparagus in a circle on top. § Dissolve the salt in the lemon juice and add the lemon peel and basil, oil and pepper and blend thoroughly. § Pour the dressing over the salad and serve as a light lunch with sliced hard-boiled eggs, tuna and anchovy fillets.

Insalata di fagiolini con il pane fritto
Green bean salad with fried bread

Serves 4; Preparation: 20 minutes; Cooking: 15 minutes; Level of difficulty: Simple

Cut the tips off the beans, cut in half, wash and cook in a pot of salted, boiling water for 7-8 minutes, or until *al dente*. Drain, dry on a tea towel and place in a large salad bowl. § Sauté the bacon in a small sauté pan with 1 tablespoon of oil until crisp, drain and set aside. § Fry the bread in a sauté pan with 4 tablespoons of oil and the garlic, drain when golden brown, and dry on paper towels. § In a small bowl, dissolve the salt in the lemon juice, and add the pepper, oregano, parsley, spring onions and 6 tablespoons of oil. Dress the salad, sprinkle with the capers and toss with the cubes of bread. § Serve as a light lunch or as a side dish with grilled meat.

> VARIATION
> — To make the salad more complete, add a simple omelette (4 eggs for 4 people). Beat the eggs with salt and pepper and cook in a large sauté pan so that it forms a thin layer. Cool and dice and toss with the salad.

INGREDIENTS
- 500 g (1 lb) green beans
- salt and black pepper
- 2 bunches chives, finely chopped
- 200 g (6½ oz) bacon, diced
- 11 tablespoons extra-virgin olive oil
- 5 1-inch-thick slices homemade-style bread, cut in cubes
- 1 large clove garlic, cut in quarters
- juice of 2 lemons
- 1 tablespoon oregano
- 1 tablespoon finely chopped parsley
- 8 spring onions, chopped
- 2 tablespoons capers

Wine: a dry white (Riesling Italico)

Insalata allegra
Summer salad greens with strawberries and apples

Serves 4; Preparation: 20 minutes; Level of difficulty: Simple

Blend the oil, chives, salt and pepper with a whisk. Set aside for 20 minutes. § Wash and dry the salad greens. Arrange a bed of mixed salad leaves in four individual salad bowls. § Wash the apples thoroughly, divide in half, remove the core and cut in thin wedges, without peeling. § Arrange a ring of apple wedges over the salad in each bowl. § Scatter the sliced radishes over the apples. § Cut the strawberries in half and garnish each salad, placing a slice of ricotta between each strawberry (if the ricotta is too soft to slice, distribute with a teaspoon). § Pour the dressing over each plate. § Serve with crunchy fresh bread or toast as an appetiser.

INGREDIENTS
- 5 tablespoons extra-virgin olive oil
- 2 tablespoons chopped chives
- salt and freshly ground black pepper
- 400 g (13 oz) lamb's lettuce or green cutting lettuce
- 200 g (6 oz) curly endive hearts
- 2 Red Delicious apples
- 10 red radishes, sliced
- 450 g (14 oz) firm ripe strawberries
- 350 g (12 oz) ricotta, sliced

Wine: a dry white (Colli Albani)

Right: *Insalata allegra*

INSALATINA DI BOSCO CON RISO SELVATICO
Woodland salad with raspberries and wild rice

Serves 4; Preparation: 20 minutes; Cooking: 40 minutes; Level of difficulty: Simple

Cook the rice in a pot of salted, boiling water for about 40 minutes, or until cooked. § Wash and dry the mixed salad greens. § Prepare the vinaigrette. Crush about 15 raspberries and add to the dressing. Blend well. § Place the salad greens in a large salad bowl (or 4 individual bowls), add the herbs and toss well. § Sprinkle with the carrot and pour half the vinaigrette over the top. Garnish with 20 raspberries. § Drain the rice, shaking thoroughly to remove excess moisture. Transfer to a bowl and mix well with the oil. § Place in a large serving dish (or 4 individual bowls) and garnish with the remaining raspberries. Drizzle with the remaining vinaigrette. § Serve the salad with the rice as a first course or light lunch, or as a main course with grilled sole or bass or poached eggs.

INSALATA DI LENTICCHIE E ODORI
Lentil and herb salad

Serves 4; Preparation: 20 minutes; Cooking: 45 minutes; Level of difficulty: Simple

Cook the lentils with the onion (with the cloves stuck in it), thyme, bay leaves and carrots in salted, boiling water for about 45 minutes. § Check the carrots during cooking and remove as soon as they are soft (which will be before the lentils are ready). § Drain the lentils, shaking well to remove excess moisture, and transfer a salad bowl. Discard the bay leaves, thyme and cloves. § Cut the onion in thin slices and dice the carrots and transfer to the salad bowl with the lentils. § While still hot, season with oil, salt, vinegar and pepper, and mix well. § Add the chopped garlic and parsley and mix again. Set aside for 5 minutes. § Serve as a side dish with grilled sausages.

■ INGREDIENTS

- 150 g (5 oz) brown rice
- 100 g (3½ oz) wild black or red rice
- 500 g (1 lb) mixed wild salad greens (green radicchio, dandelion, wild endives)
- 2 quantities vinaigrette (see recipe p. 28)
- 300 g (9 oz) fresh raspberries
- 1 bunch arugula, cut fine with scissors
- 1 bunch salad burnet
- 15 fresh mint leaves
- 1 bunch fresh chervil, in sprigs
- 2 bunches cress, coarsely chopped
- 4 carrots, finely grated
- 4 tablespoons extra-virgin olive oil

Wine: a dry red (Capri)

■ INGREDIENTS

- 500 g (1 lb) lentils, soaked overnight
- 1 large onion
- 2 cloves
- 1 sprig fresh thyme
- 5 bay leaves
- 3 large carrots
- salt and black pepper
- 5 tablespoons extra-virgin olive oil
- 2 tablespoons red wine vinegar
- 4 cloves garlic, 4 sprigs parsley, finely chopped

Wine: a dry red (Nebbiola d'Alba)

Right: *Insalatina di bosco con riso selvatico*

Pomodoro al tonno
Tomatoes filled with tuna and mayonnaise

Serves 4; Preparation: 30 minutes; Level of difficulty: Simple

Wash the tomatoes and cut a 6 mm (¼-in) slice off the top of each. Hollow them out with a knife and teaspoon (be careful not to break the skin). Place them upside down on a plate to drain for 10 minutes. § Sprinkle the insides with salt and pepper. § Prepare the mayonnaise. § In a bowl, squash the egg yolks with a fork and mix with 2 tablespoons of mayonnaise. Add the olives, anchovies, capers, tuna and parsley. Mix well, adding mayonnaise as you go. § Chop the egg whites and add them to the mixture. Keep mixing with the fork. Add pepper to taste. § Use a teaspoon to fill the tomatoes. Place a teaspoon of mayonnaise on the top of each and garnish with 2-3 capers and basil leaves. § Place the filled tomatoes in the bottom of the refrigerator for 20 minutes. § Serve as a first course or light lunch with torn lettuce leaves dressed with oil and lemon and toasted wholewheat or homemade bread.

■ INGREDIENTS

- 8 medium ripe tomatoes
- salt and freshly ground black pepper
- 4 hard-boiled eggs
- 2 quantities mayonnaise (see recipe p. 28)
- 6 green olives, pitted and finely chopped
- 6 anchovy fillets, chopped
- 60 g (2 oz) capers – 40 g (1½ oz) finely chopped, others whole to garnish
- 300 g (9 oz) chopped tuna in olive oil
- 1 tablespoon finely chopped parsley
- 16 fresh basil leaves, torn

Wine: a dry white (Montescudaio)

Insalata di pecorino e baccelli
Tuscan broad bean and pecorino cheese salad

This salad is best in early spring when broad beans are just beginning to be appear in the shops. They should be fresh and tender from the earliest picking.

Serves 4; Preparation: 20 minutes; Level of difficulty: Simple

Pod the broad beans and place in a large slightly concave dish. § Dice the pecorino and mix with the beans. Add pepper, a sprinkling of salt, and the oil. § Mix well and serve the salad as an appetiser by itself or with a platter of cold meats such as prosciutto, ham and salami.

■ INGREDIENTS

- 1.5 kg (3 lb) small, broad beans in their pods
- 300 g (10 oz) young pecorino cheese
- salt and freshly ground black pepper
- 4 tablespoons extra-virgin olive oil

Wine: a dry red (Chianti dei colli Senesi)

VARIATIONS
– Add the juice of ½ a lemon and 200 g (6½ oz) of diced prosciutto.
– Add two peeled and diced sweet pears.

Right:
Insalata di pecorino e baccelli

■ INGREDIENTS

- half a medium white or red cabbage
- 2 sweet red onions
- 1 Golden Delicious apple
- 2 quantities vinaigrette (see recipe p. 28)

Wine: a dry white (Orvieto Classico)

INSALATA DI VERZA E CIPOLLA
Cabbage and onion salad

Serves 4; Preparation: 15 minutes; Level of difficulty: Simple

Cut the cabbage in thin strips and slice the onions thinly. Toss well together. § Peel and core the apples, dice and add to the cabbage. § Prepare the vinaigrette and pour over the salad. § Toss well and set aside for 10-15 minutes before serving with barbecued pork chops or fried chicken.

VARIATION
– Replace the vinaigrette with 2 quantities of homemade mayonnaise (see recipe p. 28).

INSALATA DI GAMBERI E FAGIOLI
Shrimp and red bean salad

Serves 4; Preparation: 30 minutes; Cooking: 5 minutes; Level of difficulty: Simple

Wash and dry the salad vegetables. § Strip the red leaves from the radicchio and arrange in 4 small salad bowls. § Arrange the endive over the radicchio leaves. Chop the radicchio hearts and sprinkle over the endive. § Drain the beans and distribute in the 4 bowls over the salad. § Heat 2 tablespoons of oil in a sauté pan and sauté the shrimp with a little salt over high heat for 2 minutes. § Add the wine vinegar with the lemon peel and cook for 3-4 minutes more. § Place the remaining oil, with salt, pepper, spring onions and celery in a bowl and beat vigorously with a fork. § Divide the shrimp, 4 in each salad bowl, and pour the oil over the top. § Serve at once as a first course (prepare grilled fish to follow) or as a second course preceded by a shellfish risotto.

INGREDIENTS

- 2 large heads red radicchio
- 2 hearts curly endive, chopped
- 450 g (14 oz) red kidney beans, precooked or tinned
- 16 shrimp, shelled
- salt and freshly ground black pepper
- 8 tablespoons extra-virgin olive oil
- 80 ml (3fl oz) white wine vinegar
- peel of ½ a lemon, grated
- 4 spring onions, finely chopped
- 1 celery heart, finely chopped

Wine: a dry white
(Falerio dei colli Ascolani)

VARIATION
— A simpler version can be made with white beans and shrimp cooked in salted, boiling water for 3 minutes and seasoned with extra-virgin olive oil, salt, freshly ground black pepper, and 2 tablespoons of finely chopped parsley.

INSALATA CAPRESE
Tomato and mozzarella cheese

INGREDIENTS

- 7 large red tomatoes
- 500 g (1 lb) mozzarella cheese
- 20 large basil leaves, cut in strips with scissors
- salt and freshly ground black pepper
- 6 tablespoons extra-virgin olive oil

Wine: a dry white (Capri)

Left:
Insalata caprese

Serves 4; Preparation: 15 minutes; Level of difficulty: Simple

Cut the tomatoes in 6 mm (¼-in) thick slices and arrange on a flat serving dish. § Cut the mozzarella in slices of the same width and alternate with the tomato. § Sprinkle with basil, salt and pepper, and drizzle with the oil. § Serve as a first course or light lunch (with lots of crunchy fresh bread).

VARIATION
— For a tastier salad, sprinkle with 2 tablespoons of dried oregano.

Insalata di farro
Emmer wheat salad

Emmer wheat has been grown in Italy for thousands of years. It is used in Italian cuisine for salads and soups. Look for it in speciality shops, or try replacing it with pearl barley. This delicious salad looks even more appetising if served in a wooden bowl. To give it even more colour and flavour, add 4 raw diced courgettes and 8 crumbled anchovy fillets.

Serves 4; Preparation: 15 minutes; Cooking: 40 minutes; Level of difficulty: Simple

Cook the emmer wheat in a pot of salted, boiling water. The cooking time will depend on the freshness of the grain, so try a couple of grains after 40 minutes; it should be *al dente* (chewy but firm). § Drain and rinse under cold running water. Drain again and shake out excess moisture. § Transfer to a bowl. Add the tomatoes, mozzarella, spring onions, basil, capers, salt, pepper and oil, mix well and set aside for 5-10 minutes before serving. Put extra olive oil on the table with the salad because the emmer wheat absorbs it and could need some more. § Serve as a first course.

■ INGREDIENTS

- 3½ cups emmer wheat
- salt and freshly ground black pepper
- 16 cherry tomatoes, cut in half
- 250 g (8 oz) diced mozzarella cheese
- 6 spring onions, chopped
- 15 basil leaves, cut in strips with scissors
- 60 g (2 oz) capers
- 6 tablespoons extra-virgin olive oil

Wine: a dry white (Vernaccia di San Gimignano)

Insalata di cuori con salmone
Salad hearts with smoked salmon

Serves 4; Preparation: 20 minutes; Cooking: 7-8 minutes; Level of difficulty: Simple

Wash the salad greens and dry on a cotton tea towel. § Remove all but the pale inner leaves from the artichokes by pulling the outer ones down and snapping them off. Cut off the stem and the top third of the remaining leaves until only the tender heart remains. Cut the artichokes in half lengthwise and scrape any fuzzy choke away with a knife. Cut each heart in half and cook in a pot of salted, boiling water with the juice of 1 lemon for 7-8 minutes, or until they are white and tender. Drain and set aside to cool. § Dissolve ½ teaspoon of salt in the remaining lemon juice, add the oil and pepper, and mix well. § Place the lettuce, endive, celery, palm hearts and spring onions in a bowl and season with the dressing (save some for the artichoke hearts). § Mix well and arrange the salad in 4 plates. Place the artichoke hearts at the centre of each and drizzle with the remaining dressing. § Garnish the 4 bowls with the salmon. § Serve as a first course with toasted wholewheat or homemade bread.

■ INGREDIENTS

- 2 heads lettuce, divided in leaves
- 4 large artichoke
- salt and freshly ground black pepper
- juice of 2 lemons
- 5 tablespoons extra-virgin olive oil
- 1 large head Belgian endive, thinly sliced
- 2 celery hearts, chopped
- 4 palm hearts, sliced into thick wheels
- 4 spring onions, chopped
- 375 g (12 oz) smoked salmon, thinly sliced

Wine: a dry aromatic white (Pigato)

Right:
Insalata di farro

■ INGREDIENTS

- 10 bunches green
  radicchio
- 185 g (6 oz) pancetta, diced
- 2½ tablespoons red wine
  vinegar
- 4 tablespoons extra-virgin
  olive oil
- salt and freshly ground
  black pepper

*Wine: a dry sparkling red
(Lambrusco)*

Radicchio verde alla pancetta croccante
Green radicchio with crisp-fried pancetta

Serves 4; Preparation: 25 minutes; Cooking: 5 minutes; Level of difficulty: Simple

Discard any wilted leaves from the radicchio, trim the stems, wash thoroughly, drain and dry. § Sauté the pancetta in a sauté pan without oil (it produces enough of its own). Add the vinegar and cook until the pancetta is crisp. Remove from heat. § Season the radicchio with oil, salt, pepper and vinegar and sprinkle the pancetta over the top. Toss well. § Serve with hard-boiled eggs and toasted homemade bread rubbed with garlic.

Insalata di Carciofi
Artichoke salad

INGREDIENTS
- 5 large artichokes
- juice of 2 lemons
- 2 pinches salt and freshly ground black pepper
- 6 tablespoons extra-virgin olive oil
- 2 tablespoons finely chopped parsley
- 2 tablespoons finely chopped mint leaves

Wine: a dry sparkling white (Pignoletto frizzanti)

Serves 4; Preparation: 25 minutes; Level of difficulty: Simple

Remove all but the pale inner leaves from the artichokes by pulling the outer ones down and snapping them off. Cut off the stem and the top third of the remaining leaves. Cut the artichokes in half lengthwise and scrape any fuzzy choke away with a knife. Cut each artichoke in wedges and soak in a bowl of cold water with the juice of 1 lemon for 15 minutes. § Dissolve the salt in the remaining lemon juice. Add the oil, pepper, parsley and mint and beat vigorously to emulsify. § Cut the artichokes in thin slices, pour the dressing over the top, and toss well. § Serve as an appetiser or as a side dish with grilled meat or fish.

Insalata Cotta di Verdura Miste
Cooked mixed vegetable salad

INGREDIENTS
- 5 bulbs fennel
- 5 artichokes
- 6 medium carrots
- 6 long courgettes (zucchini)
- 6 medium potatoes
- 6 beetroots
- 500 g (1 lb) green beans
- 1 quantity mayonnaise (see recipe p. 28) or 1 quantity vinaigrette (see recipe p. 28)

Wine: a dry red (Chianti dei colli Aretini)

A classic of Italian cookery, Insalata cotta is nearly always on the menu in any restaurant or trattoria, and is served at home at least once a week. The secret lies in the dressing, either homemade mayonnaise or extra-virgin oil and vinegar (or lemon juice). You can vary the vegetables according to the season or what you have on hand.

Serves 4-6; Preparation: 25 minutes; Cooking: 25 minutes; Level of difficulty: Simple

Cook all the vegetables whole in salted, boiling water until they are done *al dente*. You can cook them all together if you wish, removing the different vegetables as they are ready. The beetroots will stain the other vegetables, so you might want to cook them apart. § Peel the potatoes and beetroots after cooking. To peel the beetroots, just press the skin with your fingers and it will slip off easily. § When all the vegetables are cooked, drain well and arrange (either sliced or whole) on a large tray, divided by types. § Serve warm with vinaigrette, mayonnaise or a little lemon juice and olive oil. § In Italy this cooked salad is served as a side dish with roast meat or fish, or hard-boiled eggs and tuna.

Right:
Insalata cotta di verdure miste

Index

Spinach
~ Swiss chard and spinach
   fritters 89
Spring onions 11
Spring peas with prosciutto
   and parsley 52
Stewed lentils with Italian
   sausages 59
Stewed porcini
   mushrooms 50
Stuffed artichokes 44
Stuffed aubergines with
   provolone cheese 68
Stuffed peppers 34
Stuffed cabbage rolls 60
Stuffed courgettes 32
Stuffed courgette rolls 98
Stuffed lettuce-leaf rolls 60
Summer salad greens
   with strawberries and
   apples 112

Tarragon 14
Thyme 15
Tomatoes 12
~ Crispy-fried green
   tomatoes 86
~ Grilled tomatoes 99
~ Tomato and mozzarella
   cheese 119
~ Tomatoes baked with
   parmesan, parsley and
   garlic 71
~ Tomato croquettes 90
~ Tomatoes filled
   with tuna and
   mayonnaise 116
Tuscan broad bean
   and pecorino cheese
   salad 116
Tuscan-style kidney
   beans 35

Vegetable broth 24
Vegetable pie 80
Vinaigrette (Salad dressing) 28
Vinegar 16

White baby onions
   braised in white wine 39
Woodland salad with
   raspberries and wild
   rice 114

Zucchini (see courgettes)